HAT TRICKS
FROM HEAVEN

*The Story of an Athlete in
His Own Prison of Addiction*

KATE GENOVESE

PUBLISHED BY FIDELI PUBLISHING, INC.

ISBN: 978-1-60414-980-7

Visit the authors website at:

www.KateGenoveseBooks.com

Some stories, like this one, need to be told. The book reveals how life's hard places need not stop us in our tracks but instead allow us to discover a deeper purpose to our lives, despite pain and loss. If the words in this book made a sound it would be the sound of creek water moving swiftly over rocks—turbulent, yet ultimately peaceful.

—Dr. Paul Coleman
Author of *Finding Peace When Your Heart Is in Pieces*

"The author has laid her heart wide open in this memoir ... joy, excitement, pain, guilt, pride and devastation. Kate has turned it into hope amongst the sadness she endured."

— Sharon W., mother of an addict

"Only way to arrest the disease of addiction, is not to pick up. If you have someone in your family that is an active addict, love that person but hate the disease; one day at a time."

— Jim Sud, 30 years recovering addict
Served in Viet-Nam-Iraq-Kuwait and Afghanistan

Hat Tricks From Heaven *is a story about life, transition, death, and rebirth. Katie takes the reader on a journey to a place the soul calls home. Each chapter will awaken the inner visions of your mind and give voice to your heart's connection with them. This book should be on the shelves of anyone experiencing grief, loss, and transition.*

— Sam Oliver, author
What the Dying Teach Us: Lessons on Living

DEDICATION

This book is dedicated to all the women, men and children all over the world who have the disease of substance abuse.

To those who have lost their lives to addiction and the countless people who have made it into recovery; one day at a time.

God bless.

ACKNOWLEDGEMENTS

Many thanks to my friends and family who encouraged me to write this story.

Geno, you will always be in our hearts, and we will never forget what a tremendous son, brother, nephew, cousin and friend you were to so many.

To my editors Andrea Cleghorn, Jeanne Freeman, Robin Surface from Fideli Publishing, and David West, my computer expert.

Thanks to my husband, Gary, who has remained the rock in my life, as we've worked at healing together since Geno's passing.

To my best friend and daughter, Jessie Kate, and her husband, Bryan, who helped me to learn to laugh again this past year.

Last but not least, to our golden retriever, Frankie, who brings joy to us every day and sat next to me while I wrote this book.

TABLE OF CONTENTS

"I will kidnap you,

raise you,

then return you to your family so

they can bury you."

— HEROIN

PREFACE

Hat Tricks From Heaven is the true story about my son, Christopher John Genovese, who was known as "Geno" his whole life. Geno accidentally overdosed at the age of 30. He was a wonderful son and friend, and people were shocked by his death.

Geno loved hockey, so the title of the book is appropriate. The term "hat trick" is used in both field hockey and ice hockey, and refers to when a player scores three goals in a single game. This usually culminates with fans throwing hats on the ice from the home stands, though I think this happens less and less often. It interferes with the ice and the referees end up picking the hats up and throwing them back at the stands or giving them to the kid who got the hat trick.

Geno got many hat tricks during his early years. As time went on, though, he had so much competition plus knee and shoulder injuries and was lucky to score at all. Geno later told me he'd had to take a few Percocets to make it through a game because the pain was terrific. If I had known this at the time of the game, I would have given the information to the coach.

I believe the reason for this book is to open parents' eyes so they will recognize the signs and symptoms of an opioid problem. If you're concerned, immediately go to the drug counselors at your child's school for advice. Oftentimes they might not think anything is wrong —they are often in denial just as I was many times — but be persistent.

Please read the story with an open mind, and remember addiction doesn't have a certain zip code. Addiction afflicts in the wealthy communities just as often as it does the lower income areas. Be aware and educated and don't hide in denial.

Love and hope to you all.

Kate Genovese

PROLOGUE

I had just awakened and said the word "rabbit" immediately. It was a significant word to say in my family of origin. The story of the rabbit goes back to a Scottish and English superstition. If you say the word first thing in the morning, as soon as you wake up, on the first day of the month, then you will be granted good luck for that month.

This was a tradition my mother taught us, and I had been following it since I was first able to speak. My kids loved this superstition; especially my son, Christopher, who had been nicknamed "Geno" since middle school. He made it a point to say the word way before his brother, Dan, and his sister, Jessie. I remember thinking, *Kudos to him! He's a step ahead of his older siblings.*

But that September morning, I didn't hear the word rabbit coming from Geno's room. He had accidentally and fatally overdosed three months before.

I got out of bed and reached for my phone. My husband, Gary, had texted me to see if I was okay. He'd called or texted me every single morning since Geno died.

"Yes, hon, I'm fine. Did you remember to say 'rabbit'?" I asked.

"Nope. You beat me to it."

He knew what I was thinking. If Geno were alive he would be the first in the family to call it out. Every month he said the word before anyone else in the family, even at the age of 30.

Although I called my son Chris or Christopher, in this book I'll refer to him as Geno. Geno is the name he preferred, and the one almost everyone had called him since fifth grade.

Geno was a happy kid, a lot like both Gary and me. He loved having the name Genovese, pretending he was in the mafia. He could imitate the Don in *The Godfather* movie to a T. His voice and mannerisms were exactly like Marlon Brando's.

He loved acting out all sorts of characters when he was in grade school. In the fifth grade, Geno played the Cowardly Lion in a close imitation of actor Bert Lahr in the class production of *The Wizard of Oz*. Geno got a standing ovation for his performance, and he thought briefly he might go into acting, but his love for hockey soon took over.

From kindergarten through eighth grade, Geno attended Woburn public schools in Woburn, Mass. After that, he was enrolled in an independent school called Governor Dummer Academy, now known as The Governor's Academy, in Byfield, Mass. He went there hoping to improve his hockey skills and academics, eventually hoping to go to a Division I (hockey) college.

He continued his education at Assumption College in Worcester, where he played all four years, minus the months he was off ice because of injuries.

His first injury was to his knee when he was in ninth grade. He tore cartilage playing hockey. In all, he would have five more surgeries over the next 10 years. Geno's doctors prescribed Percocet for post-operative pain for all his surgeries. As a result, he became addicted.

This is Geno's life story with mine and other family members and friends sprinkled in. As his mother, I loved bringing him up. We had so much fun together, just as I did with my other two children. Geno received more attention because of his injuries and his resulting addiction.

I never thought that his childlike enthusiasm for hockey at such a young age would lead to a deadly addiction to Percocet and eventually stronger opiates. It was even harder to believe that heroin would kill him at the age of 30.

He was too young, I told God two weeks after his death. *Why my son? Why didn't the jackass who sold him the drugs die instead of Geno?* We were told through some of his acquaintances that the guy was a dealer and didn't use drugs himself. But we really didn't know what the truth was, maybe time would tell.

As this story moves along, there will be disclosures — police involvement, courts, judges, probation officers and medical personal — but in the end our son was gone and we would have to learn a new way of life without Geno around.

"It will be your new normal," one of my friends told me. She had lost her son to the same disease of addiction 10 years earlier.

She was trying to be helpful but it didn't work during the initial days after his death.

Through the grace of God and many friends who love us, we are accepting his death. That's all I can say a year later, working on my emotional pain and accepting our loss.

We miss you, Geno.

...MYSTERIES BEFORE DAWN

I remember my fifth-grade teacher asking us to write down what we believed to be the largest number possible. We all diligently scribbled out long strings of digits—usually with many zeroes or nines—only to be told that no, we hadn't discovered that elusive number. "Can you add one to that number?" she finally asked. Of course. "And one more after that?" And then it hit me. Numbers went on forever. There was no end. And the universe, too, may well be infinite. And our souls. Every time I considered how some things go on forever, it seemed a mind-numbing concept to grasp. But one day I asked myself if I could imagine loving my children forever and then the concept of infinity seemed simple to understand.

Kate Genovese understands love and all that it can bring to one's life. Writing so openly about her son Geno's life and death, she explored the great mystery of existence and the perhaps never-ending search for the answer to the eternal question "Why?"

In one passage, she writes about saying the rosary right after she learned of Geno's passing, and how she was able to go through all the rosary's "mysteries before dawn." That phrase captured me. In our lifetime on this earth we all will wonder why certain things had to happen, why a loving God allows suffering, and what is the true purpose of our existence. But those mysteries can never be answered once and for all until dawn arrives—that time when the light is bright enough for us all to see clearly. Until then, we see through a filtered prism.

When reading this book it was obvious that Kate was scared for her son as he struggled with addiction. But how worn out she and her family must have been, too. When a loved one is an addict and at risk for losing his life, so much of one's waking hours is spent "doing" and there is little time for simply "being." Even when the doing is nothing more than constant worrying and asking "What if…? over and over in one's mind, it is an exhausting experience.

Most of us may never regard ourselves as heroes, yet when our life is upended and we must venture forth into the unknown and somehow persevere despite fear and even hopelessness, we are taking part in what is known as "the hero's journey." In this journey, we are called to action—and we often don't wish to accept that call even though the journey awaits us whether we want it to or not. In the early part of the journey we are like Dorothy in "The Wizard of Oz" having to walk a road that bends and curves. What lies ahead is not always possible to see or predict.

In all such journeys we learn something—about others, about life, but mostly about ourselves. We find ourselves having to reach down deep into the pockets of our very souls and pull out a new insight, a new vision, a new sense of purpose and meaning so we can trudge forward.

But the purpose of that journey is not just to learn or to have an experience. It is to learn and have an experience in order to give back. Near the end of the struggle is a sign on the road that says "Next Stop: Compassion". For it is the giving back, the teaching of others all we have learned, that we help our fellow travelers to experience some sort of comfort or knowledge that will aid them on their own journey.

Kate Genovese understands the road of compassion and the need to give back. And it is in that type of giving that her son Geno's life takes on an even greater purpose and meaning. Kate hopes and trusts that maybe one life will be saved by the sharing of Geno's story.

And I have no doubt that will happen.

— Paul Coleman, Psy.D.

CHAPTER 1

GARY, 1969

Gary and I met in an elevator when I was just 19 and living in Boston, Mass. I had rollers in my hair and my nurse's uniform on. I was on my way to my sister Irene's with my roommate from nursing school, Trisha. My sister Irene was married and had a baby at the time. Gary was headed to the same place we were, my sister Irene's apartment. Gary had a mustache. He's always had a mustache, but at the time he also had black hair down to his waist. I thought he was cute.

My sister Irene was babysitting for Gary's nephew, Tim. and Gary was there to pick him up. I was getting a couple of joints from Irene for our night out.

I kept staring at him and Trisha nudged me. "Stop staring."

"I can't help myself."

Trisha laughed. "I'm sure he's ready to jump your bones with rollers in your hair."

"Oops," I said, as I felt my head. "I forgot."

Gary and I ran into each other again in a Cambridge bar a few years later, when he tripped over my table on his way to the men's room. I recognized him right away from the elevator, and he did me, too — even without the rollers in my hair this time.

"Gary, right?

"You got it."

"How's your family?"

He looked uncomfortable.

"Hey, I'll meet you outside." I said.

We talked for a bit, he told me about his father dying and I told him how sorry I was.

I was chilly.

"Let's go to my van and warm up," Gary said, and put his arm around me.

We talked, made out and went home to my apartment. That was it. He never left.

Gary wasn't in a good place mentally since his father had died as a result of a fire in his workplace where he made furniture. His uncle, who had owned the business with his dad, wouldn't let him stay at the shop and work, so he picked up jobs here and there, but also did drugs.

I was no better. I had a job, but was more interested in having fun.

A couple of years passed and we didn't seem to be improving. Both of our families were worried about us.

We clearly needed a change. Mary, my girlfriend from high school, had moved to Denver and she offered to let us stay in her apartment there.

Miraculously, Mrs. Genovese gave us her car. She just wanted us to get our lives together, as did my parents.

"A geographical cure may work," my sister Kerry said. I looked in my father's disappointed eyes. He wanted me to continue with nursing and get a master's degree.

I let my dad down with this decision but it wasn't the first time.

CHAPTER 2

DENVER, 1973

Denver turned out to be the right move. There were a lot of transients and they all seemed to live on Detroit Street in downtown Denver. We eventually got our own jobs. Gary did construction and I found a job at Holy Name Hospital where I made a good friend, Cindy. We had a lot in common and walked home after our 7-3 p.m. shift.

Cindy couldn't believe how bad I was at directions. I always exited the hospital doorway the wrong way and when I asked someone for directions on the street they said, "You go northwest on Main Street and head south and you should be there."

I was puzzled and they knew it. Evidently I didn't know north from south! "Can you just tell me if I go right or left?"

"Never mind," Cindy said. "I understand."

She was laughing her head off. "How did you ever get around Boston?"

"People usually give left and rights for directions, not north or west. And after asking 10 people, I could finally find it."

"Maps! No map learning growing up?"

I didn't bother going into the story of how streets in Boston followed old cow paths instead of being laid out on logical grids like Denver or

Chicago. I also don't think my dad knew what a map was, we almost got killed driving in circles in Montreal.

Gary was on a softball team with a bunch of guys called The Munchies. They weren't very serious about the game and smoked a lot of pot before and after each one.

I also was on a team and unfortunately, Gary was the captain; he put me in as a catcher. I was really poor at it and he would tell me what I did wrong. I finally quit; I didn't like to be told what to do.

We New Englanders only stayed a year in Colorado. I wasn't a cowgirl by any means. Ten of us went camping one weekend. Our friends tried to show me how to put up a tent, and Gary just stood back and watched. When he saw I didn't know what I was doing, he jumped in and finished the task.

My other task was to light a fire. I did that successfully, but in the middle of the night the tent fell over. I jumped up and put on my boots, but unfortunately the fire was still on and I stepped in it. Gary had a bucket of water and tossed it on my size 10 boot.

***

A couple of times at work I was sick, throwing up. I looked at the calendar; four days late. My period was always on time. But a week later I found out I was pregnant. Gary was upset. He didn't talk to me for three weeks.

"You dope," I said to myself, "how could you have missed a couple of days of birth control pills?"

I went to a counselor and discussed my options. After considering all of them I told the counselor there was no way I was having an abortion. "I'll do this gig alone if I must."

And that was that.

When I got home from the clinic Gary actually asked how I was feeling.

"Gee, you're talking to me?" I asked sarcastically.

"Look this hasn't been easy for me either, Kate. I don't feel ready."

"Well, *I* do. I'm going to Seattle to live with Irene. I don't want to go home to Boston yet, but I need some other family around me," I told him.

"Mary's like family, let's just stay here."

"Mary is great but there are no kids around here, everyone is still partying. I need to move on and live in a place where there are families."

To me, Denver seemed to be a stopping place, somewhere to smoke weed and have a blast before we really had to grow up and settle down to adult life.

"I have to leave, Gary. You can stay, or do what you want."

"I would never leave you, Kate. It's just my fear of fatherhood talking."

While we were in Denver, my mother would sometimes call us from home, questioning when we were going to get married and asking if there was a church nearby for Sunday mass. I lied my head off, always telling her we went to a Catholic church. I could picture her at the other end of the line frowning at me, knowing I was telling her a big fat fib.

The night before we left for Seattle, she called. Irene told her our plans — she thought I'd already told her we were heading to Seattle and that I was pregnant. That is what happens in a large, dysfunctional family.

"Now you have to get married. Promise me you will when you get to Seattle. I'll fly there and help out with the services, talk to the priest."

Shit! I knew Gary would never go for that.

Where we lived, no one was asking us about that. People seemed to be more laid back. No one particularly cared if we were married. We were a couple: Kate and Gary, Mary's friends from Boston. The sacrament of marriage was not important, being good people seemed to be enough for all of us.

"I promise I'll try, Mom. I would get married, but it's Gary, he thinks what we have is enough."

I heard the click. She had never been fond of him in the first place.

I guess Gary loved me enough to follow me to Seattle, despite the initial few weeks of silent treatment following the pregnancy news.

It was a sad goodbye with Mary. She was a great friend and still is to this day.

The goodbyes were short because I was cold and nauseous. It was November. We would be at Irene and Artie's before Thanksgiving. I felt a real twinge of happiness.

CHAPTER 3

REFLECTING ON MOVING WEST

O ver the years, friends have asked me why I just didn't go back to Boston and have my child there. The truth was, I wasn't ready to face my family.

I had my issues with drugs in my early twenties and I felt I wasn't strong enough to face any more of the traditional East Coast world. All my friends were getting married, behaved properly and owned homes. I wasn't willing to live up to their standards quite yet. My parents, even though encouraging me to return home, still acted as if I was in the doghouse because of my reckless behavior in high school and beyond.

When I was in high school and living at home, my friends and I were competitive — seeing who could get what boy. Even though we were long beyond that, many of my friends were go-getters, hurrying to live the way their parents did, settling down in a way that Gary and I weren't ready for. So, we decided to stay out west, in Seattle for a while.

My sister Irene and I had always been close. Her husband, Arthur Driscoll, who grew up in neighboring Belmont, was always the life of the party. He was so welcoming to us and it seemed we never stopped laughing when Artie was around.

It was funny how one person decided to go from Belmont to Seattle, then another person would go, and another; until there was a contingent of 50 people who moved there from our hometowns west of Boston.

There we were, Gary and I, moving west for the second time, taking our common history and our love of the Boston Red Sox to form a new community in Washington State.

In a way my sister Irene had also escaped. Her first husband, Paul McGrath, came home from Vietnam emotionally messed up. Addiction got to him and he was never the same.

Irene couldn't live with the problem. She didn't want her son, Paul Junior, brought up with a drug-addicted father, so they divorced and later she married Art.

Today, Paul's problem would be more respected by society and my sister. Addiction is diagnosed as a disease and most people in the 21st century are starting to understand it. At least I hope so.

In the '60s and early '70s many men had gone to Vietnam, fought the good fight, but couldn't quite adjust to building a life in their communities when they came home.

Maybe the memories of Donny Ray and Teddy Lee, both Belmont soldiers who had died in battle, helped make the decision for Artie and his friends to get the hell out of dodge and not face the war stories. But the sadness lingered. I could see it in their faces from time to time — war stories that they couldn't let go of, and maybe wondering why they didn't die in Vietnam.

CHAPTER 4

SEATTLE, 1977

Seattle was magical. I loved Pioneer Square and Pike Place Market on the waterfront. Pioneer Square had a lot of Native Americans who were homeless. They danced and entertained there to earn money from people who were on their way to work. You would find the homeless tap dancing and playing music, trying to earn some money to live, and businessmen and women tossing quarters in a bucket; if they were real lucky a dollar would be amongst the mix of coins.

In those months before my baby was born, I would take my pregnant body to the restaurant at the top of the Space Needle where Irene worked and eat my heart out as I looked over the beautiful city.

Motherhood was fast approaching. As March of 1977 came along, I finally got frightened by the prospect of becoming a mother. My due date was just a month away.

I had put on too much weight, 60 pounds. My nephew called me "Rerun," after a chubby kid on some sitcom. I felt hurt but took it in stride, it would be my new name until the baby came. I found out the baby was breech, meaning she was upside down, with her feet headed down in the birth canal. When I went into labor unexpectedly, the doctor tried to flip her around, but had no luck turning the baby around in the birth canal.

Not only was the obstetrician unable to turn the baby, but when he looked at the ultrasound he decided to tell us he feared the baby had only one leg.

"One leg?" I screamed to my sister.

Irene immediately started saying the rosary. She was so nervous when she told Gary and saw his expression that she called Arthur to come over to the hospital; she counted on Artie to calm Gary down.

I had to ask Gary, "Honey, do you think this is punishment from God?"

"Nope."

"Then why is this happening?"

"I do know you really got screwed up by your mother's religious beliefs! No, I think we have done nothing wrong."

"Well, we are not married and having sex. That's a sin if you're a Christian."

"Loving someone is not a sin in my book," Gary said. "We're blessed, don't worry." I looked over as he continued to read the sports page from one of the Denver newspapers. The columnist's name was Woody Paige and Gary was addicted to him; he had a friend send him his column every week.

Art was a little buzzed but he showed up. In typical Artie fashion, he kept up the jokes with Irene and Gary, and occasionally the doctors would let them peek in on me. Artie sang and danced along to the Temptations in my room. But one horrible contraction accompanied by my screaming drove him right out.

Soon after that, I was wheeled into the operating room with Gary holding my hand; a C-section was necessary. He watched as the doctors made an incision and said "Wow, Kate, your insides look like tripe." Somehow, that lessoned the tension and my daughter was born, and with both legs. As Gary held her and counted all her limbs; he cried. It was the first time I saw him burst into tears with happiness.

My daughter, Jessie Kate, was beautiful. We bonded immediately even though she looked just like my mother-in-law and her sisters. I was blessed. Having her helped straighten both Gary and me out. No longer did we think of drugs; we concentrated on our beautiful gift from God. That's how I felt, anyway.

Jessie Kate was born April 21, 1977 at 12:50 p.m. Every year since she became an adult, she calls me to wish me a "Happy giving birth day," and reminds me how grateful I was that she had two legs." I truly have the most awesome daughter on this planet.

She chose to be a social worker and you couldn't find a better one. God was so good to us then, and I appreciate both her and her husband, Bryan, in my life.

***

Gary, despite his earlier reservations about being a father, was a natural. He was ready, and I felt lucky. Although I nursed Jess, Gary was right there to help: changing diapers and rocking her to sleep. It couldn't get much better!

We had her baby pictures and family pictures taken when she was a month old and sent them out. Our friends were astonished to see our new family — Gary had gotten his waist-length hair cut right up to his ears. He was a hippie no longer. He kept the mustache but the long hair was gone. His mother was thrilled to have a "normal looking" son and proudly showed the pictures to her work friends at St. Elizabeth's hospital!

The next winter the snowstorm of 1978 on the East Coast arrived. All our friends back in the Boston area were homebound and called us constantly from the front lines of the blizzard. There wasn't much they could do. The roads were all closed. No driving was allowed except for essential jobs or emergencies and it was almost impossible to walk anywhere. Our friends gradually got out on the streets as the intensity of the storm dwindled. Back at home they all talked about having meals together, making sure they got to the package store for booze. Sex definitely passed the time and several of my friends got pregnant. There were a lot of babies born nine months later that year.

I began to get homesick as a result of all those calls. I was missing the fun and my family. My parents begged me to come home; they hadn't met their new grand-daughter who was almost a year old.

I was torn. Irene didn't want me to leave and Artie loved having Gary around. The two of them were peas in a pod and Art was a big help with Jessie. He was familiar with fatherhood, as their daughter Leah was 2 and of course his stepson Paul. Paul Jr. was my favorite nephew, even though he called me Rerun!

When I was capable, Paul would race with me around the neighborhood in West Seattle. "Come on Auntie, you can do it." Evidently, he didn't want a chubby aunt.

He was also broken hearted when we decided to go back east. Gary and I were big fans of his 8-year-old soccer team and he loved having us around.

"You can visit us Pauly," I said as we were loading up our pickup.

"Can I live with you if Mom doesn't want me anymore?"

"Your mom adores you," I told him as I hugged him and looked at his big brown eyes full of tears. As we drove east I thought of my beautiful nephew, my buddy with his beautiful red hair and his athletic ability. He was an amazing soccer player at age 8.

"So long, Seattle," I whispered to myself as we crossed over the West Seattle bridge. "We'll be back to visit."

CHAPTER 5

SEATTLE TO BOSTON, 1978

In March 1978, we drove from Seattle to Boston in our white Ford 1972 pickup we had bought out there. We made the backseat of the truck cozy with a mattress and toys so Jess could play.

We were about to celebrate Jessie's first birthday. We took turns driving and banging her plastic toys to the sounds of "Stayin' Alive" by the Bee Gees.

Gary had reservations about heading east, especially when we stayed in Denver for a week with Mary and saw all our friends. Denver was magical, with the mountains and beautiful sunsets. The mountain vegetation made it look as if the mountains themselves were celebrating spring.

"Why not stay here, Kate? I mean really, the difficulties we had, some of the trouble we got in at home — maybe we should start over here? Mary would let us stay with her until we found work and a place, I talked to her about it."

"Gary, I thought we settled this?" I angrily picked Jessie up and put her in the backpack, and went for a walk. Colorado would be a great place to stay, out in the suburbs, like Cherry Creek, I thought. My husband was confusing me.

When we arrived back at Mary's house she said "your Mom called, wondering when you will be home."

I looked at Gary and Mary.

"Call your Mom Kate, we'll leave tomorrow."

Gary said this with still some hesitancy as he walked out of the room.

"You have a really good man, Katie." Mary hugged me.

"He is Mary, he's giving up what he really wants to please me."

***

Returning home to Boston, we found an apartment in a two-family house in Belmont. Life was good. I got a LPN nursing job at Sancta Maria Hospital in Cambridge, and Gary landed a job for the town of Lexington. He was incredibly lucky because there was a freeze in hiring, but there was a federal training and employment program called CETA, in which communities hired people to work for a year with the possibility of a permanent job. I prayed with my mother daily that Gary would be picked to work there full-time. I remember being up on my Mom's porch, sitting in our rocking chairs, Jessie in my lap, saying the rosary as I prayed that Gary would land the job.

***

Just a few months later, in July of 1979, Gary was given the permanent position in the Lexington Water Department where he works to this day. I don't know how we were talked into getting married, I guess because everyone was asking us when it would happen. But on December 8, 1978, a Justice of the Peace came to our house in Belmont for the nuptials, pronouncing us Man and Wife.

***

Soon after Gary started his job I found out I was pregnant again. Our son Dan was born in November of 1979. We bought a house in neighboring Woburn that year, an affordable city, about 38,000 people and a 20-minute drive from our parents.

***

Woburn is a great community for bringing up children. Dan, an extremely handsome little boy (here I go again like any mother) was extremely smart, energetic and athletic. He had a bit of psychic ability. When we went to visit my sister in New York he was around 4 years old. He came into her house after playing with my nephew Mike- he looked at me and said "I had to come in, there is bad energy outside."

"What kind of bad energy, Dan?"

"Cats, big cats that will attack me and Mike" He looked so scared we called Michael in; 15 minutes later there was a group of coyotes or some other creature searching the area.

Animal control came and claimed there were not only coyotes, but foxes around.

"Told you Mom" then Dan simply went back to a game of Kids Monopoly with Michael.

***

In 1980, when Jess and Dan were still small, I went back to nursing school to get my RN at Somerville Hospital. It was a tough decision, but I was now working at Lahey Clinic, a large medical center north of Boston and they encouraged LPN's to go back to school for their registered nurse diploma. Somerville Hospital had an accelerated program. I could have finished in two years going full-time, but it stretched longer as I needed to do it part-time.

During that time, in 1980, when I decided to go back to school, my mother offered to babysit three days a week.

I had a brother, Barry, in his early 30s who lived with my parents. I always had to check and make sure Barry wouldn't stay with my kids; I knew he shouldn't babysit because he had some mental disabilities. He had no patience and if he were with the kids for more than an hour some kind of altercation would ensue.

Mom agreed not to let Barry babysit and told me she would be with them at all times. I know she thought I was making a big deal out of nothing. But she promised she wouldn't leave them alone.

***

About a year later, through the family grapevine, I heard that my Mom frequently left the kids for an hour or two with Barry.

***

My father was big in politics in Cambridge and Watertown; he was on so many committees I couldn't keep track. My dad often didn't want to go alone, so off my mother went, leaving my kids with Barry, "Uncle Bub."

***

When I caught her coming in the house one day, there was no getting around it, she had left the kids with Barry. I saw it for myself.

"We agreed Mom, no Barry.

"Mom, he is not dependable and he is mean to Danny. Promise me it will be you or Dad with the kids, no Barry." She reluctantly agreed but I knew it was time to find new sitters.

CHAPTER 6

GENO, 1985

It was now February of 1985. I had five months of nursing school left.
I made fish sticks for the kids and let them sit in front of the TV and eat, a treat for them. I put them to bed at eight after reading them their favorite book—and mine, too—"Goodnight, Moon."

I had a glass of wine around 10. My mother would be calling soon. She called every night to check on me and the kids and to ask if Gary was working.

It was snowing and I was overwhelmed and tired.

My mother knew I was crying when I picked up the phone.

"What's wrong Katie-boo;" that's what my family called me now and then.

"Anna told me I am away from the kids too much. I think she is right."

Anna, Gary's mother, was old-school Italian. She typically kept to herself and almost never commented on our marriage or family life, but today she had.

There was silence on the other end of the phone.

I think my mother agreed, but she didn't say so.

"Maybe I can come over your house instead of taking them to a sitter?"

"No, I only have five months left and Kathy is doing a great job; the kids love her.

Kathy lived across from me and was my best babysitter and a friend through work and school.

"Goodnight, Mom, I'm going to go check on how much snow we are getting."

"It's supposed to be a whoppa!" my mom yelped.

I laughed, "You sound so much like your friends from North Cambridge—WHOPPA!"

We both laughed hard. My parents were both true Cambridge people. My dad, being from the worst side of town, loved his cronies and the way they spoke. Pronouncing an "r" was a sin around that area.

As I put on my coat and boots Gary called.

"Hey Babe"

"What's up, kids in never-Neverland?

"Yes, I was going to go outside and check the weather and make a snowman."

"Alone?"

"Yes alone, I'm not going to wake the kids up."

"Well, we're supposed to get 5-10 inches, depending on the way the storm goes."

"OK Don Kent," he was our local TV weatherman on WBZ TV; Gary could imitate him to a tee.

We said our good nights and I headed out the door.

I danced around on the front lawn that night, singing the song I'd just been playing, my favorite "Midnight Train to Georgia."

***

Out in the snow that night, after listening to "Midnight Train to Georgia," I thought of when my brother-in-law Arthur singing that song to me over the phone in Seattle.

I had had Jessie only three weeks before but I was so depressed. I called Irene and Artie answered. He heard the sadness in my voice.

"I'll be right over," he said.

True to his word, Artie pulled up to my house in a flash with the song blaring, and getting out of the car he danced with me and Jess on the front lawn — my favorite brother-in-law of all times—always having the ability to cheer me up.

What a memory that was. Irene and I would tease him — every ounce of him was Irish but he could dance, spin and sing like any of the Motown guys. We often joked with him that he was born to a black family in his past life! Lucky Arthur. Seriously!

***

I looked up at the snowflakes; it was still snowing, but slowing down. I guessed Gary would finish plowing around 2 a.m. and check his routes. He'd be home in a couple of hours.

"To bed I go," I said to the partially hidden mystical moon. I finished the one glass of wine I allowed myself and hopped into my cozy bed. I loved having the bed all to myself and I drifted off to dreamland.

The dreamland didn't last too long. I heard Gary brushing his teeth and washing his face, but quietly. He opened Jessie's door and kissed her cheek.

(If he wakes her up I will ...)

Then he went into Danny's room and soon I heard the two jabbering away. But Dan would go back to sleep. He was the world's best sleeper. I thought, "Thank you, God."

Gary came into our room—I was drifting back to where I had been near-dozing about 20 minutes before, trying to get back into the dream I had before Gary came home.

When I went back to sleep I continued the dream I had been having about our family 10 years in the future: Gary and I were 44, Jess, 14; Dan, 12. Our family had a beach house in Wells Beach, Maine. The kids were older and trustworthy, so I could take a long nap on the beach and if they were hungry, off they'd go to the clam shack and leave me alone sleeping. In reality, of course I never got a minute to sit on the beach; there were sand castles to build, swimming on the boogie boards with me and the constant hitting and fighting because Dan stole the shovel from Jess and I had to break it up. But in this luxurious dream I could nap for as long as I wanted because of the nanny I brought along. (*I was really dreaming big. There was also a housekeeper to make sure the house was cleaned and dinner all ready, bottles of wine opened as we were having guests, and the menu was lobster, clam chowder, corn on the cob and hot toasty bread.*)

I reluctantly came out of my dream with Gary shaking me.

I was still half-asleep and wanted my dream back.

"You're drooling." He was laughing and handed me a tissue. "Having your lobster dream again?" I threw the pillow at him and curled up in a ball trying to go back to sleep.

I peeked out of one eye. 5:30 am. I had two hours before the kids would be all over me. I was going to enjoy every one of those 120 minutes and rolled onto my side of the bed, intending to go back to the beach I was dreaming about.

Gary wrapped his arm around me; I ignored him. He moved closer, pushing against me.

"Really, honey?" I said. "The kids will be up soon and I need sleep!"

"Come on Kate, it will help me sleep; you know how restless I get after working all night."

I felt another nudge. "Please, hon."

"I don't have my diaphragm in, and by the time I get it…"

"Shush, Kate," he kissed me. "Stop worrying for once."

Afterward, I stayed still in the bed and wide awake, Gary was snoring but looked peaceful. I immediately had the gut feeling I was pregnant; there was going to be a third kid.

Or did the sex really even happen? Maybe it was a part of the dream that we made love in between the lobster dinner and dessert.

I looked at the clock. It was now 6:15. I turned and looked at the bedroom door; Danny was standing there, as cute as could be in his Red Sox pajamas, wearing his matching baseball cap. His big green eyes stared at me.

"What was all that commotion about?" he asked.

I laughed, trying to think of a G-rated reply.

"The sanders, sanding the roads to make people safe when they are driving, they make a lot of noise." Even my five-year-old was skeptical.

He held up a monkey book he loved. "Can we read it now?"

I signaled for him to climb in bed beside me. We looked at the pictures for a minute or so, then I looked over at my Dan and he was snoring. The two of them, just alike. I quietly got out of bed and looked out the window and saw the snow was only a few inches deeper. Gary had been out several hours plowing, they wouldn't call him back again.

I turned on the TV checking for school cancellations and I heard "No school for Woburn," the announcer said. That meant pre-schools too, so our kids could sleep—what a treat.

I made coffee and waited to get a call from the phone chain saying I didn't have to go out to nursing school myself. But no luck. We had patients, after all.

I sipped my coffee as I put on my student uniform and left Gary a note. I added a postscript.

"P.S.," I wrote. "I don't want my brother Barry babysitting if you get called to work" and gave him Kathy's number.

My mother-in-law was probably right about leaving my kids too much. But it would soon be over, just five months left of nursing school, then I would only have to work at Lahey Clinic three evenings a week.

"God, please let everything be okay with the Genovese family until June. No catastrophes, injuries, deaths — nothing, please!"

Then I thought of the few hours earlier when we had had unprotected sex. I looked at the calendar. Hmm, we had cut it close, but maybe I'd get a break. I laughed to myself.

"Very unlikely." I was one of eight children; my Mom had my sister Denise at 48!

I gathered my books and backpack full of work clothes for my shift later. I wouldn't see my family until midnight.

CHAPTER 7

JOURNEY OF JOY, 1985

I told Gary I was going for a pregnancy test at school. The lady that worked in the clinic was very cool, no judgment at all, she always said it was part of life.

Her name was Peggy but everyone called her Pegs or she wouldn't answer.

So, as I walked near Pegs' office, I saw a woman coming out with two kids crying and yelling at her as if she caused the pregnancy.

Then in the waiting area, I witnessed her refusing two teenage girls birth control pills without their parents' consent. I didn't think that was the rule but I had to mind my own business.

I walked in. "A normal one finally" as she looked me up and down, Or not so normal?

"I'm late."

"How late?"

"Two, maybe three weeks.

She drew blood and then had me hop onto the table for an exam.

"Will this be your third, if you are pregnant?"

"Yes."

"Do you want to keep it?"

"I never thought otherwise."

"Adoption, abortion—"

"I'm good, Pegs. I have a good husband, we'll weather the storm if I am pregnant."

She removed her hand and said, "I think you are, Kate. Let me go check the blood test."

I was fairly calm. I knew I was with child without anyone telling me; that's what the Native Americans did, they just waited and knew.

"Let's flip a coin," she said as she brought out the test result and a penny.

"You are mean — no coin flipping."

She smiled. "You are pregnant, Kate."

"Do you want to stay and talk?"

"No, I'm going to pretend like everything is normal….go to classes and then home."

She gave me a hug, "Good luck."

I did neither. I drove to Watertown to see my mom. The 9' o'clock mass would be over and she was probably making a batch of cookies for the next set of grandchildren to arrive.

She heard the door open, "Hello, anyone home?"

"In here, is it you Katie-boo?"

She saw the look on my face.

What's wrong?"

"Nothing."

"You skipped class to tell me nothing?"

"I'm pregnant, Mom."

She came over and gave me the biggest hug. I could feel tears on my neck.

"Another of God's children comes into the world."

"I knew you'd be happy, that's why I came here first."

"Gary, you don't think he will be happy?"

"It's not that, it's just more stress for us, we're flat broke — good thing school is out in five months; I better pass the nursing boards."

"You will, God has been so good to you to grant you another child. Look at the girls we know trying to have kids and they can't."

My mother left for a minute and then came back into the room.

"I was mailing this today, it's the rest of your tuition for nursing school, the less money you will have to worry about."

I hugged her tightly. "What a gift, what a gift," I thought.

My Mom looked right in my eyes and said "Don't forget, the joy is in the journey."

I smiled. "Another one of my Mom's Scottish sayings. "Meaning what?"

"The journey of life, there is a lot of negativity as you travel this world God presented to us; but there is an awful lot of joy!"

"So, the joy is in the journey of life Mom, I get it."

"But barely. I was 34 years old, struggling financially, beginning to think my kids didn't know me because I went to classes every day and worked three nights a week- intimacy with my husband was infrequent in this past year yet there was supposed to be joy?"

I never said any of this to my Mom, I thought it on the way home.

On the twenty-minute ride home, I thought I was being was selfish. Where was my appreciation?

But it was there when I got home. I was a bit late. Gary locked eyes with me as I pulled into the driveway. Jess and Dan waved at me through the window and probably went back to a cartoon show. Gary was sweeping the excess snow in the driveway.

"Sorry I'm late."

"It's okay, hon." Gary looked at me with his chocolatey brown eyes, waiting for me to tell him the results.

"The test is positive; we're having another child."

"I knew it the minute it happened," he said as he put down the shovel and gave me a hug.

"Pegs said we have choices."

"Who the hell is Pegs?"

"A nurse who works in community health, it's her job to give us options."

"Not in this house! The only choice is having it — having a third kid."

"I should have thrown you off me, you big lug."

"Come on, another hockey player."

"Could be a girl."

"Girls play hockey now, Babe."

"I don't want that. I want her to have dancing lessons; ballet and tap."

"Oh, right, like you, when they kicked you out of dancing school because you tap danced too intensely and you hung your tongue out too long and the audience was more focused on your mouth."

"Who told you that?"

"One of your sisters, I guess."

We were both laughing when we went inside to tell the kids. They were ecstatic for a bit, but then they each asked where the baby would sleep.

"We don't know if it's a boy or girl yet, but at first he'll sleep in our room, 'til he or she gets a bit bigger."

"I hope it's a boy! I want to take him in my room and change his diapers," Danny yelled, jumping on the bed.

"We're moving ahead kids, Let's celebrate with some pizza for supper!" Dad yelled.

And so, it was a new chapter, or I should say another chapter for 1985.

CHAPTER 8

GENO'S WAKE, JUNE 3, 2016

The first person to arrive at the wake was the pizza shop lady who had her restaurant near Assumption College. She was clearly heartbroken.

"Geno came to see me every day, even if it was just to talk," she told my sister Irene.

"Boy, did that kid like to talk," she said. "I think I know the story of your whole family. I gotta tell ya, did he ever love his parents! It took me over an hour to get here, I don't know Woburn, not sure if I was ever here, but I felt Geno guiding me in the right direction. I don't know one student who didn't love or respect Geno."

Irene told me she wrapped her arms around the pizza lady, forgetting her name; but just hearing she loved him and he visited her daily, and drove an hour or so to give Geno a last goodbye! "That is true love, like he was her son," Irene said.

Renie cried at the thought of it, and would always remember the conversation.

A cousin I hadn't seen in a while came in and gave me a hug.

"I lost my son last year. He was 42 — heart attack."

"How awful."

"I have the memories, and in time you will, too."

But I always had memories written down, if something fun happened with one of the kids I would jot it down and leave it somewhere in the house and I would find it at some point and stash it with others in my memory box.

My other cousin, Bobby Flaherty came over to me. "You'll be all right someday, Kate, just not today." He had lost his daughter at an early age. I had to believe him, I would move on eventually into a different phase of loss, yet love would stay.

I was in a daze as some people came through the line. I remembered just wanting to end the night, to go home and hug my husband. Instead, I excused myself and went to the ladies' room. On the way there I peeked at Geno in the casket and I thought about the nine months I carried him.

I had been a very healthy, very happy pregnant woman 30 years ago. I ate well, drank very little alcohol. It was back in the day you could have one or two glasses of wine, but I didn't do too much of that. I kept up my running, four or five miles a day. I never felt sick at all, just extreme happiness that Gary and I had made the right choice.

Studying for my nursing boards were the hardest thing to do at six months pregnant. I kept thinking I was going to flunk them and asked my nurse manager Mary Mann if she would keep me on as an LPN.

She would just shake her head and laugh. I would jog off my anxiety about the prospect of failing, but in the end, all went well. The girls at work had a big cake to celebrate. Geno kicked from inside when I took the first bite.

I wished I could have lived part of our lives in Denver, and maybe Geno would be having a pick-up game of hockey that June night instead of lying in that casket.

Or maybe we should have stayed in Seattle and the kids could have played soccer, which was a big sport in Washington.

I heard a knock on the door, "Kate, are you in there?"

"Yes," I said, through tears.

"You need to come out, people are looking for you."

"OK, hon, right there."

CHAPTER 9

FAMILY OF FIVE, 1985–1991

Geno was born on November 5, 1985. He was 6 lbs. 9 ounces and had beautiful olive skin. My parents had sneaked in my room in the hospital; my Dad, thrilled to have another hockey player was extremely happy; my mother on the other hand said "Isn't God listening to my prayers; we have enough grandsons in the family, I wanted another girl; but oh well, as she bent down and kissed his furry cheek.

I was half asleep when I heard my dad say "furry cheek."

"Stop that John, he is beautiful and his cheeks are not furry."

"But they are, Mary, a lot of Italians are hairy, 'furry,' as we called them in East Cambridge."

My mother thought I was still pretty medicated; I peeked out at them having this conversation.

"Nope, not my grandson; look at him, he already has Katie's smile and Kerry's dimples."

Yes, my sister Kerry would be thrilled; she bonded with my son the minute they locked eyes, so I am told. And she did have great dimples.

It didn't matter — Geno, Christopher then — was mine and Gary's and we just looked at him, like our other kids, thanking God he gave us such gifts — furriness and all!

The nurse told me at Mt. Auburn hospital that I bonded with him well. He actually didn't want to be taken from me to be washed. That was comforting to hear.

A week later we were home. Geno was in a basinet in our room when Gary jumped onto our bed. He was wrestling with Jess and Danny.

"I'll be a good brother, I promise," Danny said. "I'll sing to him if he doesn't sleep."

"We know you will, that's why we will move him into your room when he is a little bigger."

Gary was a great dad. We were living on Garden Street in Woburn, and before supper all the neighborhood kids would play street kickball with "Mr. Rogers," Gary's nickname. Geno sat in his little bassinette on the lawn and listened to all the commotion. His big brown eyes lit up and he was kicking his feet, wanting to get out and play sports with the rest of them.

But only two years had gone by when Geno knew he wanted to be out there on the street with the big boys, kicking the ball around, learning the game.

Geno wanted to get on the ice fast. He watched Danny play goalie and he would practice with him in the driveway.

We felt our house on Garden Street was getting too small for us. The rooms were tiny and there was a six-year age difference between Dan and Geno, not ideal for sharing a room.

We thought of adding on another bedroom, but one day looking at the newspaper I saw a colonial house on Whispering Hill Rd on the west side of town.

I called my mom and asked her if she'd like to take a ride with me.

We called the realtor, and had a look-through that day.

The house was big, with four bedrooms, living room, dining area and den. The highlight was the backyard—it was huge. We had no yard at all at the house where we were living, the area behind the house taken up by a pool. That pool on Garden Street was a tremendous amount of work.

I called Gary and he looked at the new house, trying to find things wrong with it because he didn't want to leave our neighborhood.

"Gary's right, Katie, these kids will be grown and gone in 15 years and you'll be stuck with a big house, just the two of you," my mother said.

Gary smiled at my mother; I think that was the first time he agreed with her.

But I got my way—we sold our other house quickly and moved in the late spring.

Gary had torn some ligaments two days before we moved; he leaped out of the work truck and his knee buckled. But he handled it well, hiring a truck and all his friends from the Department of Public Works in Lexington showed up to move the furniture.

One of Gary's friends, Lee Ferrebee, came with his little son, LeeLee to play with Geno, two little boys rough-housing around outside. So cute.

But this house was different. All four bedrooms had four different terrible colors: deep purple, bright green, dirty baby blue and the last, what the guys nicknamed "the brothel room," with red and white brocade wallpaper and red closets and of course red shag rugs.

One of the guys, Mike, was carrying up a chair when Gary yelled, "Put it in the brothel room."

The two little boys overheard Gary and followed Mike.

LeeLee, being a bit older, asked Mike what a brothel room was.

Mike laughed, "It's just a silly word your father made up, LeeLee."

But they had to go in and discover it for themselves.

Geno whispered something in LeeLee's ear and they both laughed.

The boys went over to Gary and said, "Geno wants the brothel room."

Everyone burst out laughing.

Gary swung Geno around. That's me and Mum's room, you get the baby blue one, we'll fix it up real nice!

Geno tried to negotiate in bratty two-year-old fashion but didn't get his way.

Moving to a bigger house and yard was wonderful!

There were so many kids in the neighborhood. Tim and Josh Clark. Kevin, Chris and Korey Keene, later our yard filled with kids Geno met in elementary school; Tim, Chris, Scotty and Yano.

Those were the days of cookouts, then the group of them walking to 7-11 with our son Dan supervising to get Slurpees, no trouble ever.

Gary and I both had to work a little more, a little harder to afford our new house; it was worth it. Quite a bit of money was starting to go to sports, mainly hockey for Dan and later for Geno. But the kids chipped in when they could. Dan and Jess made money shoveling in the winter and Dan with the paper route; he seemed to want to pay his way. Eventually Geno did the paper route parade but he ended up getting so involved in hockey and baseball, I was doing the paper route. Still, those were days I would never regret. And Jessie kicked in, too. She had her own cheerleader events and some girls' hockey. I really felt life couldn't get much better.

CHAPTER 10

GENO'S WAKE– JUNE 3, 2016

At Geno's wake there were more than 400 people, everyone saying kind words, some crying, and I heard friends could not bring themselves to come into the funeral home because they were broken up.

His teachers from elementary, middle school and high school came. I was surprised because it had been so many years since he graduated from all of them. But Geno had made an impression. His smile and personality were contagious. He was recognized at Gov. Drummer Academy for his hockey successes and despite his many injuries, he kept on playing.

Ms. Murphy came and Mrs. Dines, his elementary school teachers showed up.

Their pain was evident that night; how could Geno be dead? He wasn't the type to die of drugs, I was told by one of his high school friends.

I tried hard not to leave the line of people greeting Geno; but I ran to the bathroom and vomited and cried, then vomited again. My heart ached; I didn't particularly care if I lived.

I was sitting in the bathroom when my sister Kerry came in and sat next to me.

Kerry had lost her son Casey to addiction six years before. We hugged.

"How do you get over this, Kerry? He was my love, my youngest, I love him as much as Jess and Dan, but Geno somehow loved me more than the other two kids."

Maybe the nurse at Mt. Auburn hospital was right, we had a connection unlike the others.

"We better go back in line Kate, people want to see you," she told me.

Standing in line at the funeral home I saw his friends from Top Gun, an independent hockey league he played on during his middle school years and many of the parents came as well. How grateful I was for my son to be so honored and it brought me back to those playful years, the bittersweet years and the stories that came out. Seeing a bunch of the team members made my heart ache.

Why couldn't Geno be with those kid at someone else's wake, why my son?

I really didn't mean what I was thinking. I didn't want anyone to die of addiction.

But it happens. A lot .I'd heard that all the members of a hockey team from Peabody, Mass., just north of us, used heroin and only the goalie survived.

I excused myself and went outside to be alone. I was shaking, my stomach felt hollow; I loved my son so much I would have died for him so he could live! Let me be in that casket; I'm older, I've had a good life. Geno was just beginning his.

Oftentimes, Geno would go on Facebook and tell me how successful his friends were and how many trips they were taking and their salaries were six figures.

I would look at him angrily when he talked like that. "Stop looking at Facebook! It can be depressing if you aren't doing well, it will make things worse for you. You do have to start at the beginning, but you will catch up if you try, Geno."

I was caught up in my thoughts and heard a voice — it was my sister Irene. For a brief moment I thought Geno was alive; I was tired and confused and the medication I was taking was making me sleepy. Irene wiped my tears, put lipstick on for me; we were playing house I thought, like we did when we were 7 and 10, using my mother's makeup.

"You can leave, you know, we only have another hour to go."

I suddenly pictured my mother when my Dad died — very Scottish, very stoic, no tears. That was my mother Mary Carver, the very essence of her

"Nope, Rene, I'm going to pull the Scottish card and get myself back in line." And I did survive with the help of my husband on one side and my four sisters taking turns standing at my side as hundreds of Geno's friends came to pay their respects.

Random thoughts came to me as some of his grade school friends arrived. They all looked like they were 10. They were the same handsome faces, but now they were in their 30s.

It must have been hard for them, I thought; Yano, Chris, Timmy and Scotty were his friends since kindergarten, playing T-ball. Mr. Galante was their coach, and he was the best. The kids never stopped laughing, and 25 years later he was standing in line to pay his respects.

There were reminiscences; How Geno marched himself to the principal's office, telling Mr. White that his fourth-grade teacher was sexist because she always chose the girls over the boys. I had remembered that anecdote..

Geno told me how Mr. White asked him what sexist meant. Geno told him that his mother used that term all the time, that men get things in life when women don't and the women don't get paid enough!

I laughed when the principal called and told me.

"Well, he is somewhat right, I use that term so he will appreciate women AND NOT TAKE ADVANTAGE OF THEM because of his gender."

Geno and I had a very close relationship. He could just about discuss any issue with me without embarrassment; but he knew when to stop when I looked into his big brown eyes. He knew he needed to stop.

My good friend Lois handed me a cup of coffee and my friend Kathy whispered to me that the line to see Geno was out the door and around the corner. She smiled: "He was so loved, Katie."

CHAPTER 11

GENO GROWING UP, 1987–2000

Geno played the Cowardly Lion from the "Wizard of Oz" at the Reeves school in the fifth grade.

It was a stifling hot June night in 1995 and he had on the hottest costume of all. But he pulled it off. The outfit was amazing, made by Louisa Clegg and he had the voice of Burt Lehr, the original cowardly lion. He was the most popular kid in school for about two weeks, but time moves on and he realized he needed to fight hard to be the best. That was his personality.

The best hockey player, soccer and baseball player. But hockey was his dream. This was the year he was officially known as Geno; I am not sure why or why I didn't know! I still called him Chris till the day he left this earth.

Geno was not naturally thin. He battled his weight all his life, fighting to stay in shape. It wasn't easy keeping up with his friends. Most of them were toothpick thin and would make fun of him. Geno never stood for someone putting him down and he put that person right back in his place! He realized early on, around the age of 7, that he would put on weight easily. He didn't get picked for the number one hockey teams because of his weight and how the pounds slowed him down. His weight was up and down between the ages of 7 and 14, when it stabilized, then he was in shape until about age 26.

***

I thought back to when Geno was two to three years old. This being New England, we had a Dunkin' Donuts at the end of our street, maybe every street within a mile radius (the stereotype does hold true). We went at least three times a week, the two of us would walk down to Four Corners and plunk ourselves on the swivel stools at the counter and order. Geno would get a few munchkins, which is what they called the donut holes, and chocolate milk and eventually beg for more.

I was an easy mother in some ways — one more munchkin wouldn't be so bad, would it? He raced his friends, climbed hills, rode his bike; why not a delicious extra chocolate munchkin? But one day, sitting and talking to the staff there, he started to bellow, and saying there was blood on the munchkin. "Don't worry, Geno, you probably just lost your first tooth." He cried even harder. Was I a bad Mom because I didn't tell him you lost your first tooth then pooooph! The second munchkin came; and along the way, I told him that the tooth fairy appears would put money under the pillow. (I had heard of friends putting five bucks for one tooth. "They can't be serious," I thought to myself.)

The next day we appeared at Dunkin Donuts with the waitresses handing him a different kind of munchkin but Geno wanted, no needed, that first tooth he lost. He was becoming theatrical when Kerry, his favorite waitress, appeared with a fresh munchkin and a fake tooth she bought for 20 cents.

What fun the two of us had there in the early mornings.

***

My son became extremely involved with ice hockey within the next few years. At one point he didn't make the team he wanted, The Braves, an independent hockey team. He came home crying after the tryouts.

My husband handled that one. It was the classic father-son talk, the gist of it being that life doesn't end if you can't play hockey. But in Geno's case, he wanted to give it his all. My son did blame it on his weight and he became serious; if he wanted to make it to the NHL he had to drop the pounds!

***

When the hockey season started that following fall of 2007, he called up other coaches besides his own and asked to practice with them. Of course. They seemed to like Geno and his perseverance, including the attitude he brought with him about losing weight.

I would wake up on a Saturday morning, expecting to make him breakfast and see him jump in to our neighbor's truck for Mr. Keane's team's practice; he did this every weekend and even on school nights.

He got stronger, lost weight and by sixth grade became a good hockey player. That was the year of his first hat trick.

Gary would sit with the fathers watching the game in the stands and I would be with the moms, drinking coffee and most likely talking about PTO (parent-teacher organization) meetings and the current popular TV show of the day. But we would frequently look at each other when Geno made a good play, hoping for a win for our team. Geno finally made the Braves team because of his love of the game and a lot of practices.

Sunday night games were at dinner time, 6 or 7 o'clock at the O'Brien Ice Rink. The rink served the best clam chowder around and we would grab cups of it and sit there watching our sons and talking. Suddenly I heard my husband Gary yell, "Move your feet, move your feet." I looked up and Geno had scored. It happened two more times that night, the last goal of the night. What a win, what an ending!

Gary and I looked at each other and smiled — Geno's first hat trick. We both felt very proud. It hadn't come easily for him and he certainly deserved a few hats thrown on the ice. Geno gave me thumbs up as he was getting off the ice.

Unless you are a hockey player's parent, it is hard to describe when your kid gets their first goal. In our case we all felt triumphant, especially because he got two more goals, making it what is called in hockey a hat trick.

Hat tricks are not easy to get and the goals dwindle as other interests and distractions come into a young player's life, but for that moment the whole family was totally ecstatic. (We parent's sometimes needed to hold our feelings in as we didn't want to be looked at as snobs.)

I remember when I was in ballet/tap class as a child at Ms. Janet's in Belmont, she would emphasize not to brag.

If something you did was exceptional you would stand there and bow- once. That was it. I never got the chance to bow as I was asked to be removed from dancing school in the third grade because I hung my tongue out of my mouth when I danced and it interfered with the other dancers and audience.

I remember my Mom feeling sorry for me but she understood Ms. Janet.

"Don't worry Katie-boo, Ms. Janet is just a bitch, you'll get other opportunities in life." I think that was the only time I heard my mom say a swear word. I felt proud of my mother that she stood up for me. And when all my friends walked to Ms. Janet's class I would walk with them and stick my tongue out at her, as if to say "ha,ha,ha, you old goat!"

CHAPTER 12

HOCKEY, HORMONES, GOLF & HAT TRICKS, 2001-2006

Hockey was Geno's life until seventh grade when the hormones kicked in. Suddenly girls started hanging around. Geno had a good group of friends, mostly hockey and golf buddies. His friendships seemed to be around the guys until seventh grade when the hormones and girls kicked in.

They'd travel in packs to the movies or walking around the neighborhoods, looking for some excitement. All the boys would have different girlfriends every week; it seemed innocent and fun, so far.

Memories of my own came rushing in as I thought of Watertown where I grew up. There was a big hill called Palfrey Hill, smack in the middle of Watertown. We use to hang around during the day, play cards, and walk around below to Victory Field where there were tennis courts and a track, just a lot of laughing and seeing what boy would like us next. And if we were lucky, we would meet at night at Palfrey, a group of us and once again play cards and make out with our boyfriends. It sounds boring but we had fun; walking to Friendly's and buying their signature milkshake, what they called a Fribble; sipping on it until it was gone.

Of course one of the guys would get into a fist fight and we'd be cheering for the west side of Watertown against the east side.

We didn't have the sports in the late 1960s like the kids do today, nor did the parents have the worries.

A bunch of us, boys and girls would venture into Harvard Square and watch the street musicians, we were all for them making money!

Geno learned how to play golf from my brother John. John would take him up to his house on a golf course in Eastman, N.H, and gradually teach him the basics of the sport. John loved all his nieces, nephews and of course his own son Andrew, but Geno was the only one who really took to it. Right away he grasped the game and loved practicing what John taught him.

My brother was generous with his time and money, patiently teaching him the game. John had started playing as a youngster and caddied since he was 10 at Oakley Country Club in Belmont. He was passionate about the sport and passed that enthusiasm on to his nephew. So, Geno split his time between hockey and golf and his skill at both games grew, with several caddying days thrown in.

The summer Geno was 15 my brother John held a tournament called *The Uncle Open.* My nephews spent the weekend competing with each other, not only in golf but with pool. There was a nice pool table in John's cellar. I know there were a lot of laughs and the consumption of large amounts of healthy food.

To this day, John is the chef of the family. When we are invited to his place in New Hampshire, John still waits on us hand and foot, cooks the meals. Dinner is the one meal he puts his heart and soul into, though. It really deserves a photo.

But of the two sports, hockey was Geno's primary love. In seventh grade, an independent hockey team called Top Gun noticed Geno. I guess this would be called the big leagues of 13-year-olds. The coaches, Peter, Mike, Doug, and a former Bruin, who had a son on the team assisted in coaching.

At the beginning, Geno was not the best on his teams but playing for Top Gun helped him improve and he became very competitive. Over the course of his middle school years, he had several more hat tricks. He started out with the position of forward and loved watching the puck go by the goalie smack into the net. It was fun watching all the players hug each other when there was a goal.

Geno was dropping the weight and was working out and eating right. He managed to be on three hockey teams which were Woburn's town team, the Braves and the latest Top Gun.

Gary and I were torn with our own priorities for Geno. We knew school should come first, but he kept up his grades, made money by caddying, and chipped in to play on the three teams.

One school vacation Top Gun traveled to Sweden to play other European teams. My husband went with them. When they came home I thought they both acted as if they had died and gone to heaven. To this day I hear wonderful stories of that trip to Sweden.

None of this was free. Hockey is an expensive sport and Geno grew fast; he was always needing bigger shirts, better skates, safer helmets. It is not a poor man's sport.

Sometimes Gary and I had to take turns on the out-of-state trips because of the expense. I went to Lake Placid twice, once with my older son Dan's Woburn team and with Geno's Braves' team.

Let me tell you, parents do party! That is one skill we will never forget.

There were long weekend trips to Montreal, Quebec, which were some of my best memories. It was worth my extra shifts as a nurse and Gary's working more than 60 hours a week as a laborer for many years.

But we did it for the love of our kids. My daughter Jess was never left out, she came along and hung around with the sisters of the players. Even if the team came home without winning, we all still had a good time.

My mother was right: The happiest years of life are when you are bringing up your children up, or at least it was for me until we were forced to make changes.

CHAPTER 13

A NEW SCHOOL?

In January of eighth grade, Geno was approached by a few hockey coaches from the Independent School Leagues (ISL). If he was accepted, he could not go to Woburn High School, but a private, independent school instead; it was a big decision.

Geno asked me what he should do. I said, "Pray," and meant it. God is the one who was really in charge of his life, all of our lives, as far as I was concerned.

He rolled his eyes at me.

"When do I have to tell them I want to go?"

I told him the process. Apply to a school, interview, have a tour of the campus and go to some of their hockey games and don't act like a thug!"

"What's a thug?"

"Look it up in the dictionary or online; then, you will never act like a thug if you want to play professional in any game."

I know, it was a sort of lie, but I needed best behavior from him going through this process.

"I have one request."

"What, I can only imagine."

"Girls. I won't go to an all-boys school."

"Of course not; you take after your father and your brother when they were your age!"

45

We both laughed.

I told him the story of Danny going for an interview at Belmont Hill; an all-boy, kind of elitist, wealthy school.

Dan had borrowed a friend's suit. I knew it was all boys and I thought Dan knew as well; I was wrong.

He made himself look extra handsome with a colorful tie and matching shirt. He did his hair just right.

Gary had gone with him on the interview and he had a wonderful tour of a magnificent school.

But the teacher showing him around pointed to everything male-related; sports, classes, lunch. Danny excused himself to go to the men's room, inside there were the students talking. Dan asked.

"So where are the girls' dorms?"

The students were kind enough.

"It's all dudes, dude!"

"Really?"

One kid shook his head. "We have dances twice a month with an affiliate girl's school."

Danny told me the story afterwards; he couldn't stop laughing,

"What normal guy would go to this school Mom? I'd lose my mind not being able to look at boobs all day!"

"Gee, Dan, thanks for sharing," I said sarcastically.

"Many boys your age are focused on careers; their dads or moms were doctors, lawyers, scientists. Thinking about the opposite sex isn't their priority."

"Sorry, Dan, I guess we should have discussed this before the interview."

"I'm okay, Mom, a learning experience, right?"

***

The next few months were filled with hockey for Geno, watching the school's hockey games, buying a suit for the interviews (another few

46

extra shifts) and not dismissing the fact that he might go to Woburn High and to talk to Jimmy Duran, the hockey coach at the time.

Geno did. Jimmy came over our house and talked about Woburn's hockey record and how it is improving academically.

Geno and I were so torn when he left, we both cried, seriously, that is how bad we felt thinking about his leaving the Woburn school system.

Geno told his Woburn friends of the potential change in schools. They were shocked; they wanted him to stay, be part of their group, but when he received the acceptance letter from Governor Dummer Academy he decided to give it a chance. I think he was influenced from some of the Top Gun players, as they were all going to private schools.

This change could possibly mean eventually getting to enroll in and play hockey at a Division I Hockey college. That is what I was told by so many coaches and parents that had been through the ISL (Independent School League system.

His official acceptance letter with its big packet of information and the cost came along with it. How could we, as parents decline? He was practically attending this school for nothing.

The next five years would be a rollercoaster ride for Geno and our family; we had no idea what God had in store for all of us; but it was good to focus on his first year; ninth grade and Geno's expectations.

CHAPTER 14

GOV. DUMMER ACADEMY

Geno moved into Whitney Hall as a Freshman at Governor Dummer Academy in 2001. He had a great roommate and his house resident assistant was Jeff Wotton. Wotty, as the kids called him, was also the athletic trainer and Geno loved him. As usual Geno tried to get away with things when he got in trouble. But I considered Geno's trouble as just kid stuff, not really serious.

Sneaking out of their dorm at 3 am; borrowing golf carts and riding them around with another student in the middle of the night, of course getting caught with detention to follow; he also missed some classes from time to time and was found in the girl's dormitory where his girlfriend lived. He took his punishment well and learned his lesson, but the school did take his behavior seriously.

The house representative asked me if he ever had any "incidents" in middle school, any trouble we as parents were concerned about.

"Nothing," I responded.

But did I answer too quickly? Geno may have had a dark side somewhere. He had a few fistfights with other kids, confronted teachers occasionally, but mostly he was a solid kid as far as I could tell.

Geno reminded me of myself when I was in ninth grade at a Catholic school.

There were no serious events in my case, but enough that the nuns decided to keep an eye on me, watching my behavior, then telling my parents I wasn't Catholic school material. With any luck that wouldn't be Geno. I wondered if he should have stayed at Woburn High School.

GDA's football coach Mr. Gerry saw potential in Geno as a lineman and then a fullback in Geno's freshman year. I begged him not to play football. I wanted him to concentrate on academics first, then hockey. To me, that seemed to be plenty.

But my husband had played football when he was in seventh grade right through high school, so he encouraged Geno to get on the team. I was hoping he wouldn't be picked seeing he was a freshman; no such luck. I tried to convince him not to play, but he didn't listen to me; he was learning to love football as much as hockey and he wouldn't give up either. His father wasn't worried that he was doing too much. His attitude was to let him play, because if he loved it and was good at it and did his best, it was important to let him have fun.

"Mom you have no idea how much fun we have playing football and in the locker room, I might decide just to play football and give up hockey."

"Well, then make up your mind, hockey or football." But he loved both and I didn't have the emotional strength to make him choose.

Halfway into his freshman season he tore cartilage in his knee and had arthroscopic surgery. Surely this would be the end of it. Wasn't this a sign to quit football when the season ended in November?

Oh, no. He recovered from the surgery and finished the season.

But there was something else going on, something wrong with Geno that I couldn't pinpoint. One of his football coaches mentioned to me after practice one afternoon that Geno looked like he was in "outer space," not paying attention to what was happening on the field. "His mind is somewhere else" as he put it. "Maybe something is bothering him."

"Well, he did have surgery and this is a new school" I said to the coach. I will keep an eye on him when he comes home on weekends."

It was easy to tell when something was bothering my son. His usual cheerful mood, his usual hugs and occasional "luv you Mom" would stop.

He avoided me when I came to visit and seemed angry I was there. But of course, he was with a group of friends, including girls, why would he want to be with his mother?

It was an Easter celebration when he came with us to my husband's family in Cape Cod. Jessie and Danny weren't able to join us, so it was just Gary, Geno, and me on a very long, two-hour ride to Harwich.

He was silent with music pouring in his ear and texting away to his friends; this wasn't my son, he barely looked at us.

I couldn't stand the silence when we pulled into Gary's aunt's driveway.

"What's wrong, Geno, this isn't you, I know something is up!"

"Wrong! There you go Mom, reading into things; I'm fine."

"No, you're not; since Christmas I've noticed a change in you and so has your coach."

"You're making that up" he said angrily.

"Now Kate, really?" Gary said as he got the cooler and dessert out of the car.

"Can this wait?"

Gary was great at avoiding issues and I was the opposite, I wanted to find out what the problem was and find a solution. Yes, I definitely was a helicopter mom at times. He had always been so open with me, now I felt like he had dived into a cave and would stay there until someone dragged him out of the living room, or the cave.

"Five minutes, hon, Geno and I will meet you in there."

I watched Gary go to the door, his cousin greeted Gary and I waved, "We'll be right in Bobby."

Bobby waved in acknowledgment.

"Okay Geno, I know kids change when they go to high school. God knows I did, I avoided my parents as much as I could. But this feels different."

No reply.

"Do you want to go to Woburn High?"

He contemplated what I had said, then shook his head.

"That would be giving up. Dad told me once I start something I have to finish it."

"I think Dad is referring to sports, getting a job, things like that. If you want, you have my permission to go to WHS to be with the friends you grew up with."

"I'll give it my freshman year, then we'll see. Deal?"

"Deal. But what the heck is bothering you?"

"Mom, I just don't want to talk about 'issues,' as you put it. I'll work things out by myself."

He said this with a sadness in his voice, his big brown eyes looking at me, welled with tears. He simply looked sad.

I am a hands-on healer. I am a Reiki master who places hands on people and help them get well. It is a wonderful concept. I have helped many clients with this practice.

When Geno was in middle school he loved me to do Reiki on him; it helped him, he would talk and tell me his seventh-grade problems that seemed so minor now. I could never approach him now about Reiki; middle school, yes, high school a big no. He was at the point he thought it was foolish.

Was I worrying too much?

I thought about my mother, unlike me she didn't seem to have any worry genes in her head. She was always singing or humming from the minute she got up until bedtime; I remember the song she loved and would sing it at the top of her lungs:

"Que sera, sera, whatever will be will be, the future's not ours to see, que sera, sera."

My dad would look at me and smile, shake his head, probably wondering how he married a continuously happy person. Eventually he told me not to listen to her advice, "she isn't always right kitten."

"I'll think about my problems tomorrow," my mother would say, and tomorrow would come and she was on to a world of denial of issues and sure only happiness would come her way. She was a good catholic, went to church daily and followed all the rules of the church. God would never let anything bad happen to her family.

But I could hear her sing that song, over and over in my mind. I missed her, even though I knew she was wrong some of the time, she was still my mom. But why couldn't she see the problems of the family?

There was my father's drinking, but mostly it was my brother Barry's behavior. Barry needed help for his mental illness. I knew he was strange, different, but my mom saw him as a beautiful little boy, curly brown hair, big green eyes, and good at golf. He got lots of trophies and went to caddy camp every summer. He was perfect, according to my mom, who denied all my life that my brother Barry had problems.

***

As the year went on, Geno seemed better. His knee healed and he started baseball in the spring. It wasn't his favorite sport, but he enjoyed the camaraderie. I liked that it wasn't a contact sport.

I enjoyed watching baseball; sitting in the stands on a cool afternoon in the spring, just wearing a light jacket and feeling the beautiful sun pouring down on us in the stands. I started meeting some of his teammates' parents: I found out that my son didn't want to use his name Chris; he preferred Geno.

"Way to go, Chris," I called out early on, when he made a good catch.

"His name is Geno," one of the mothers corrected me.

"I'm his mother; his name is Chris" I said laughing; I didn't want any fistfights in the stands.

My friend Sara Morrissey laughed.

She had two sons at the school; J.J. and Brian. We became good friends.

"Everyone here knows him as Geno, Kate."

Boy, have I had my head in the clouds, I thought to myself.

"Gee, Sara, I thought they stopped calling him that after fifth grade."

But I guess not; he always introduced himself as Geno, I think it reminded him of the fifth- grade play, when his popularity grew.

I didn't realize the nickname stuck with him, but, really, in the scheme of things it was no big deal.

Geno finished his freshman year. He was home with us for the summer. He hung out with his Woburn friends a lot and seemed pretty normal to me.

Later he told me he had started drinking and smoking some pot by then, but I was blind to it at the time, until I saw him smoking weed in the backyard.

I could smell it and confronted the four kids out there with him. They were very stoned; I remembered the days I had smoked pot continuously for a year until I realized I was losing my memory when I did it. I was in nursing school and I realized the dangers and quit, there and then.

The four boys looked at me in wonderment. They looked paranoid then they all burst into a 10-minute laughing fit.

"Shush," I said, looking around to see if neighbors heard us.

"Let's talk about it."

"I'm not mad, guys, just wondering what you get out of smoking pot; it made me paranoid."

"You got high, Mrs. G?"

I laughed. "In nursing school, my two roommates were potheads so I tried it; but I ended up stopping because I would get paranoid, thinking everyone was talking about me!"

They all laughed, relating to my story.

"Everyone drinks, Mom, I started with my Woburn friends but Casey and I smoked pot and drank when we went away with Auntie Kerry and Uncle Kenny last summer."

"In eighth grade, Geno? Terrific."

"Yeah, well, come on, Mom, we're teenagers."

"No more in this house guys, off limits; it is the gateway drug."

The boys were still stoned and burst out laughing.

"Hanging around with the DARE officers Mom?"

I stared at my son, a glare that told him to shut up.

"I don't know what to say, other than drugs aren't good for you and alcohol is just as bad; Geno, if you get caught on campus it is lights out for you." I looked at his other friends.

"I'm sure Woburn has some punishments, too."

It ended for Geno for a while. He worked caddying and played golf on his free time. Some days I questioned if he was stoned, but decided to just watch, not make a big deal of it.

My nephew Casey was starting to use drugs more frequently; Geno often tagged along with him. My sister Kerry was concerned after I talked to her about it.

Neither of us wanted to make a big deal about it, yet we didn't want to ignore it. Both in high school, it could get worse and we would have to keep an eye on them.

But Geno was great for the rest of the summer; continuing to make money caddying, mowing lawns, and doing various odd jobs, so he had some cash and still asked me for more. The manipulation for money was beginning, but I didn't realize it right away.

"Can we get this straight? You're asking me for money, yet you are caddying, landscaping and helping out with roofing?

He was a manipulator, as most addicts are; he turned the scenario back on me. He insisted he was trying to save money for new hockey equipment and he had to pay for books at school.

Yup, I fell for it. He would play me against Gary, and both of us would give him some money. I fell for it more than my husband, later on realizing some of the money would go to booze and pot. But Geno could be sincere. He would come home from a day of caddying and give me some money to put away for him; we had a joint account, and if he needed money the rule was he had to ask, and he did all through high school but eventually life changed and he was sneaking money in his college years.

It was my fault. I didn't notice or check our joint account. I trusted him. No news is good news; but I was as sick as he was, I didn't realize the progression of his illness. Addiction was beginning to take over, becoming the powerful monkey on his back that he wouldn't be able to get rid of.

CHAPTER 15

A DREAM, JULY 2016

Geno had been gone for two months and I had a dream. Geno was showing me that his knees didn't hurt anymore nor did his shoulder; he was swinging a golf club without pain, and he was pointing to his knees, showing me that the cartilage had healed and he could play golf in heaven without pain.

Gary gave me a little nudge, but it didn't wake me. He knew I was dreaming.

Geno was smiling in heaven, he was on the golf course; he looked in his early 20s with people I didn't recognize. But he was laughing, and before he knew it, his golf ball made it to a hole in one!

Then before I knew it he was playing hockey and I kept seeing him scoring, one goal after another. It made me so happy I didn't want to wake up.

His uniform was an old pea coat from the 70s and It buckled up the front — no protective gear like we have here on earth. But why would you need it? No getting hurt in heaven!

And his face was so alive and intense which was how Geno looked playing hockey, the determination on his face as he knocked players over as he headed down the ice to reach the net and score. He was taught to perform at 100% whether he played offense or defense, it was his job to score. I remembered my son Dan's face, as a goalie the intensity as a puck was coming near, he had great movements and when he made a save he almost didn't want to celebrate because he was waiting for the next puck he had to save. And Geno, he was intense because he wanted to score, get that puck in the net for the team.

Maybe it was just a dream, but I have had psychic abilities all my life and I wouldn't dismiss this one. He was in heaven or on a heavenly plane or a new dimension that was foreign to me.

I was getting a message that his pain was gone, the terrible pain he lived with for many years from sports injuries. No denying it, it was confirmed by doctors, especially his shoulder pain. So, Geno was on another planet free and happy while our family was suffering from his death. But we were from a strong Irish-Scottish heritage and of course the wonderful Italian blood on the other side of the family.

When his friends were in line at the wake there were comments from some girls that Geno helped them in their own relationships, acting as a counselor and guiding them to the right decision.

One girl who went to Assumption with Geno said she was walking back to her dorm one night from the library. Geno heard screaming and ran over to see a guy trying to accost this girl; "Geno saved my life; I could have been raped or killed, but once Geno pushed the kid off of me and he ran because he knew Geno could waste him."

"Wow, did you report it?"

"Yes, we went to the campus police and told them what we knew but they never found him. Geno walked me to my dorm and told me to get pepper spray!"

I had tears in my eyes; she handed me a tissue. "He was the best, Mrs. Genovese."

There were plenty of the guys who showed up saying what a good captain he was in high school and college and saying wonderful things about his GDA years and Assumption years and how memorable they were; some of their eyes were red, they had been crying but Geno told me once in middle school that hockey players don't cry and were told to keep a stiff upper lip.

"Where did you hear that crock of sh…"?

My coach, when I was a "mite." (The hockey team for kids 6- to 8-years-old.)

"Well, I don't agree. You may not want to bawl your eyes out in front of the whole team, but crying is important, it lets out your feelings."

But I have to say, when he was at GDA and had a bad game he would start to well up and his dad would hug him and head for the men's room. "Get it out, you'll feel better" Geno would come out with dry eyes and a different outlook. Gary has been a fantastic father and I know Geno respected that, and learned it was normal to have a good cry from time to time.

CHAPTER 16

SOPHOMORE YEAR, GDA–2002

After a lot of conversation, Geno decided to go back to GDA for his sophomore year. Gary and I helped him get settled into the sophomore dorm and all the kids seemed happy to see him.

He had to get to football practice so we said our goodbyes. "See you on Saturday for the game." It would be a big one. They were playing Belmont Hill, which had a great football team.

It still felt weird to have him at boarding school. The house felt empty. There was no teenager making a mess or playing floor hockey with his friends. It really took getting used to, trusting the teachers and dorm teacher to watch over him.

I am sure there are a million stories Geno could have told me, but I only heard some of the funny ones. At the same time, there were questionable ones that caused the dean of students to call parents.

Geno and a friend noticed a freshman who had gotten drunk before a campus party. They tried to help the kid and watched over him all night, covering up for him because it was his first year there. The next day, he and his roommate were found guilty of getting the kid drunk because the campus police found liquor in their dorm. I guess the GDA police had searched the room without Geno knowing about it.

More detention. It was something that shouldn't have been blamed on Geno and his roommate. The school made them separate and get new roommates; it was probably a good move, as the two of them shared a reckless energy, but they were so sad they had to separate, they felt like brothers.

***

I could tell Geno was angry at something but he wouldn't let me into his secret world. Gary didn't notice it, or he was in denial.

We had gone for a visit and took him to Mike's Restaurant in Newburyport.

Geno silently ate his clam dinner and kept looking at his watch; we took him home earlier than we had planned.

On the way home, I told Gary I was concerned, his behavior once again was scaring me.

"Let it go Kate, he's a teenager."

"That's right, a teenager who will get tossed out of school if he doesn't smarten up."

But he had hockey and football. Jen Downey, his girlfriend at the time, seemed to be keeping him in line. She was a good girlfriend for Geno; witty, smart and she cared about his well-being and ended up going through a few tough years with him.

I can't quite remember when the injuries fell into place. It seemed with each sport he hurt his shoulder or a knee, the doctor prescribed Percocet after the surgeries, even though I frequently asked the doctor to stop; especially since he had been taking a narcotic for over three weeks after his shoulder surgery.

"Addiction runs in my family," I said to the doctor.

"Geno isn't an addict," he said firmly to me. "Stop hovering over him."

I felt ridiculous at that point; I wasn't hovering, I was a concerned parent.

Geno tore cartilage in both knees playing hockey. Two more surgeries and he was out for the season in his junior year.

He had to sit in the stands and watch the games with the other fans; but he had a lot of friends and Jen, especially cheered him up.

Jen was awesome. She had a great sense of humor and helped Geno through his injuries. Her family also took him on some trips which helped. The Downey family was from Europe and they believed in a lot of laughter, which helped Geno when he was in slings, on crutches, and in pain.

I don't know if I ever thanked them but I certainly wanted to. They lived in a wealthy part of Wellesley and they were generous with their home.

I went over several times and would get lost in their enormous house. On one of the visits I intended to thank Jen's mother for her generosity and kindness, but when I came out of their many bathrooms I got lost. I was twisting and turning as I was trying to find my way, wishing I had my phone with a GPS. Finally one of Jen's friends found me wandering.

"Are you looking for Mrs. Downey or Geno?"

"Either one, I'm lost."

We both laughed and he took me to the Downey's outdoor pool.

There were too many kids and adults around to thank her for loving my Geno; so I will say it now. *Thank you, Downey family, for being so kind and generous. I will never forget you!*

***

During the summer of his junior year (he repeated his junior year, so this was his second time around) he worked at Boyle's, which was a gym for athletes. He did well and was able to play sports for that entire year without needing surgery!

He played as a defenseman in hockey and in football he switched positions. When his left shoulder popped out of his socket a team member just pushed it back in and Geno kept on playing!

I will never understand the athlete's mind. If I had done that to myself I would have curled up in my bed for the rest of the season.

But not Geno, he taught the kids on the teams to shove his shoulder back in its socket so he could continue to play. I am not sure if the coaches knew it and ignored it because they needed him, or they were just oblivious to it all, and looking for that next goal or good tackle in football.

CHAPTER 17

JUNIOR YEAR AT GDA, 2004

In Geno's junior year I received a call from his English teacher, Mr. Greyson. He was disturbed at what Geno had written for an essay. The assignment was to be a composition on some event that happened in his life or someone else's life that had affected him and how he had dealt with it.

He went on to say that Geno had written about a dysfunctional family (not his, supposedly) where there were three children who were all sexually abused by their uncle.

"Oh my God."

I didn't want to hear the rest; my hands were shaking and I felt as if I might faint. But I heard myself say, "Continue."

"Well what disturbed me, Mrs. Genovese, is that Geno said that the perpetrator went to a hospital for the mentally ill. Joe, the main character, was so upset he sneaked a gun into the facility late at night and shot Max, the abusive uncle, in the chest three times.

As he did it he said, "This first bullet is for my sister, the second for my brother and the third, right in the heart, is from me."

I was silent. If the English teacher could have seen me, he would probably have rushed me to the hospital.

I felt as if my blood was seeping out of me and I almost fell walking over to the kitchen chair.

"You okay, Mrs. Genovese?"

I interrupted him and acted as if things were okay. I certainly didn't want him getting involved in our family life.

"Quite a story," I said, taking some deep breaths.

"Well, either Geno has quite an imagination or he has a lot of anger seething inside from something personal that happened to him or someone he knew."

"I'll talk to Geno, but would you send me the story, please?"

I told him I would discuss this with my son, and we hung up.

It wasn't easy getting ahold of Geno. He knew something was up by the tone of my voice message. Finally, he called back after Gary screamed into the phone to get home.

Geno called back and asked if we could go there instead.

Gary and I met him at his school library.

"What's up, Katie," he said in his fake-cheerful voice.

He had a bag of ice on his shoulder.

I told him what Mr. Greyson said.

"So, I wrote about a messed-up family."

"Whose messed-up family?"

Gary's beeper went off.

"Take it honey, it's okay," I said.

He came back; I knew it was a work call and he'd do anything to get out of this conversation.

"Water break?" I asked, which was a typical public works emergency.

"Two of them. They need me, Kate."

"Go Dad," Geno said. "We're almost done."

Gary kissed us and left.

It was like pulling teeth getting my son to tell the truth. Finally, he couldn't stand all the questions and gave in.

"It was a family member, a babysitter I think, it's still vague, Mom, but I remember it happened."

I walked over and hugged him, then his phone jingled. It was Jen asking if she could meet him.

I was crying.

"Please Mom, I'll be okay."

"You're not okay, but enough for tonight. What's wrong with your shoulder?"

"Skateboarding this afternoon, no worries. Wotty took me for X-rays, no more damage."

"Between your sports injuries, and the car accident this summer and now this. You'll be dead by the time you're 20 or in a wheelchair for life."

We laughed as we saw Jen walk in. She was such a sweet girl, she'd certainly cheer him up or get him in shape.

He said she was tough on him in sports, she wanted him to be the best. He called her Downey's Boot Camp.

I watched them walk away, I called after saying I would phone him tomorrow.

I was all alone in the library. I sat at a table and just cried, cried my heart out.

The tears wouldn't stop and I felt that my God, the God I believed in all my life had deserted me.

The tears were coming fast and furious. I didn't want them to stop; it was cathartic.

Then I felt a tap on my shoulder, maybe my guardian angel here to rescue me?

No, but close. A very kind and gentle librarian put her hand on my back, she whispered "We need to close, give yourself a few minutes."

She handed me some tissues. Five minutes later I was out the back door and in my car.

CHAPTER 18

END OF HIGH SCHOOL YEARS

Geno continued to have so many sports related injuries, mostly from football. Several sports related people told me injuries were a part of the world of athletes.

But the injuries seemed excessive. He had five surgeries during his high school years. One of them was related to falling off a skateboard and dislocating his shoulder, which eventually led to two surgeries on his left shoulder.

And of course, it wasn't just the injuries. It was the pain medication that came along with these injuries. As far as I could tell, I was the only person aware that he might be taking too many pills.

This was Geno's last year of high school, his fifth year.

We had a heart-to-heart talk about sports and injuries, relating to more pain medication. He wanted to play at least one sport.

"If that's the case Geno, concentrate on hockey and quit football!"

"Are you crazy? I love football and it helps with my anger."

"Are you still seeing the therapist?"

"Yes"

"Helpful?"

"Embarrassing."

Geno had finally admitted it was his uncle that abused him. He knew he had to try with the therapist to say who it was that touched him inappropriately.

We were in his dorm room, sitting side by side on his bed; he wanted privacy.

"It wasn't your fault, Geno, you were a kid. He was an adult."

"He should go to jail," Geno said as he put his hands to his face. He was crying, not wanting me to know.

"He will, it is the legal process that is taking time." I had wanted to wait to tell him that his sister Jessie filed charges against their uncle.

"So, Jess pressed charges?"

"She did, I was going to wait and tell you."

Geno started to rub his knees; he had some over the counter pain medicine that he applied but it didn't seem to help.

"I know you are trying to hide things from me, but really, Mom, I needed to know, and I did know because of everything I overheard when I was home. Besides, Jessie talked to me about it. It is embarrassing having an uncle that is a molester. At least I have one normal uncle — Johnnie is the best."

"He is a great uncle to you and brother to me; yes, we're lucky to have him and Carol in our lives."

"Auntie Carol is awesome; she looks like the movie star Diane Lane."

"Nice compliment Geno, I will tell her."

Geno was done talking, he hated to hear that his sister was affected as well by their uncle.

"I really need more narcotics for this pain."

"Will you take Motrin, please? Percocet comes with Addiction."

"But it works so well on the pain and I have to be honest, my brain as well; it wipes out the memories of…"

One of the students knocked on his door.

"Hey, Geno. Warm-up time soon, coach told me to get you."

"Next time you see Mrs. Jansen, I'd like to go."

"No! A big fat no. Maybe Dad, but not my Mom."

I gave him a kiss. "Make the appointment with Dad then. Okay?"

He shook his head. I could tell he was thinking, "Who wants to discuss sex stuff with his mother and his therapist? That would be weird."

He grabbed his gear and yelled "Bye, Mom. Lock the door behind you."

I remember thinking to myself, *This kid will be okay. Sometimes he acts so normal, such an amazing teenager. Then, for what seems like no particular reason, he isn't the son I brought up — so angry and hurtful.*

"I love you, buddy!" I yelled down the dorm hall.

"We love him, too!" yelled a few classmates. We all laughed as we were walking out the door.

Yes, he did seem happy a lot of the time. He had a lot of friends and a steady girlfriend through most of high school. He was handsome and popular and it looked like he was enjoying a great social life. Still, I knew instinctively those demons were there, ready to attack when he stopped playing sports.

Quite often he was angry with me. The summers of his high school years, he wanted to stay at Jen's home. Her parents allowed him to stay and they traveled quite a bit, even on semester breaks if he didn't have hockey. I felt he had adopted them as his new parents.

This family could afford to treat my son like a king and I am grateful he had them in his life to this day, but back then it felt like they were taking over. I still wanted him at home to do things with us, his own family; I was still his mother.

Jen's family could afford to treat Geno like a king, what teenager wouldn't want that; but he was my son and I wanted him home; he couldn't run away forever.

Gary and I wanted all three of our kids to develop a work ethic, and we didn't want Geno to get used to everything being handed to him with no effort on his part. Geno was practically living there and I didn't like it. But when he did return it felt to me that the demons of the abuse came home to him as well. The situation was troubling.

Counseling ended after a year when he refused to go any longer. Sports helped his mental health more and he played on summer hockey leagues until he graduated, despite the injuries.

"Can you take a break from the sports, kiddo?" I asked him.

"Are you crazy Mom? That's what keeps me sane and out of trouble."

He had a couple of skirmishes with the Woburn police in high school. Once the cops found pot in his car after a hockey game but he was let off the hook.

Another time, at Christmas, he and his friends were driving around town in Geno's car and they noticed a display of large plastic reindeers on the lawn of someone's house. The four boys jumped out and put one reindeer on top of the other, as if they were having sex. Of course, the boys thought this was funny, but the owner was angry and got Geno's license plate number and called the police.

We reminded Geno and his friends that this was trespassing and they needed to take this seriously, even though once again there were no charges.

Geno's high school years were bittersweet for me. He was happy yet unhappy and I felt responsible because not only was the perpetrator from my branch of the family tree, I felt my brother would end up in psychiatric care for the rest of his life. That was really bothering me. I was letting my mind go crazy; I was picturing my rotation in nursing school at Metropolitan State Hospital. It was the summer of 1984, hot as hell and no air conditioning in the building, shame on the state of Massachusetts — the poor patients! But I was thinking the worst. I remember caring for a young girl, maybe 20 who was abused by her father. She couldn't seem to move on from the incidences of the abuse and was re-hospitalized for the last five years. She would walk around in circles with her fingers in her ears because her father, in her head, was blaming her because he went to jail for the crime.

She was hallucinating and hearing voices so frequently that she continued to put her fingers in her ears to stop the sound — the sound that refused to stop.

Now, 30 years later, I had wondered if Geno would end up like this; but he didn't, he could function in life. But he had so much anger inside. Most people didn't see it because he hid it, oh, he hid it well. Somehow he controlled the post traumatic pain of the abuse by talking to a select few individuals and working out his anger with sports.

CHAPTER 19

HOCKEY COMMITMENT

My husband was so quiet and patient with Geno. He loved the life out of this kid and was always there to support him. If something was really bothering him regarding sports or his injuries, it was his Dad he went to. On the other hand, I was the sounding board and the imaginary dart board. My therapist told me to just "put up your baseball mitt and let him yell, it's good he is getting it out."

"What does that mean, put up your baseball mitt?"

"It's a saying, let him yell and scream at you without hurting you emotionally by putting up the imaginary mitt; letting all the painful words go into the catcher's mitt, not letting it get to your head. It will toughen you, let you know you're not the cause of all this."

But it made me feel like a failure as his mom. Looking back, I think I loved him too much, gave in too easily because of my guilt. After years of therapy I found out none of this was my fault. His sports injuries, his abuse, even his temper I was not to be blamed for.

But it took 18 years before I could get a grasp on not being the guilty one. I think every mother on this earth would understand. We mothers were the go-to person and we would protect our children, but in Geno's case, I had no idea what happened to him when I left him with my mother who left him with my brother. I wasn't aware back in the '80s that my son, all my children, would be abused by a family member.

Geno was at GDA for five years. He was so hoping to go to a division one hockey school, but the injuries and competition prevented it. There were so many good hockey players in New England.

At one of his last hockey games, a Division I school coach came out to see him play.

He started to do well, then, his shoulder fell out of its socket as he was hit against the boards. He limped off the ice for the personal trainer to take a look. I could just imagine how Geno felt; this was the end, there would be no other chance; it just wasn't meant to be.

I saw the scouts leave at that point. The scout called him the following week; he told him he may have a chance if he healed and did a year of junior hockey.

His dad discussed it with him. The decision was to move on to college, a division II school that would be easier to get into. It became OK with him, as he was sick of surgeries and maybe he could heal over the summer and play hockey at Assumption College in Worcester, about an hour's drive away.

I did feel bad for him and us as well. We had spent so much time and energy with his sports and he loved them. Hockey was a long season, September through March. Gary had devoted so much time, doing most of the driving in the early mornings. Gary was disappointed and so was I, but we knew Geno could not handle more surgeries, pain, and rejection of Division I colleges.

That winter he applied to several colleges and met with the coach of Assumption College in Worcester; he was a good coach and Geno liked him right away.

He spent the summer of 2005 at home. He worked doing roofing with our neighbor, Kevin Keane, who owned his company. He became the Geno I knew before he lived at Governor Dummer.

He was happy and cheerful that summer and had lots of friends over from Woburn, high school friends and people he had worked with over the years.

I thought all was status quo, but one day I saw him taking some Percocet that hadn't been prescribed for him. Bells went off for me and I was scared he might get on this rollercoaster ride of addiction. He made light of it and said he still had pain, residual pain from the last surgery.

We had a discussion but it went nowhere. Geno was going to do exactly what he wanted to do.

CHAPTER 20

ASSUMPTION COLLEGE, 2005-2009

Geno lived at the dorm the first two years at Assumption. I knew he was smoking weed and drinking some beer, but didn't suspect Percocet so much because he wasn't playing hockey on the off-season. I didn't realize how much pain he was still in with his knees and shoulders. And how much emotional pain along with it.

"Is hockey worth an addiction?" I asked him directly after seeing him high one day when he came home.

"Pleeeease Mom, I am not an addict, I am in pain."

"Then stop hockey now, Geno, addiction runs in the family, you get injured then you follow by the need for narcotics. Do you have any idea how I would feel when I saw you get banged against the boards and your shoulder came out of the socket? It was like I was experiencing the pain myself. I can't stand it. Then your knees, too! You'll have arthritis in your 30s, is this really worth it?"

"Hockey is the only thing that keeps me from thinking of the abuse. I'm just so angry all the time—hockey helps me get it out."

"You can go back to therapy; join a gym, anything but this contact sport that keeps you hostage."

"Been there Mom, done that all through high school; I need hockey, it is my savior."

Tears came to both our eyes. I think we both finally knew what was going on here. I walked away wondering and praying to God that he would come to his senses. If he could just find another way to deal with the anger from the event from his childhood and stop playing hockey.

I was working as a school nurse for those years. But the tuition at Assumption was pretty steep, even though Geno did get some free money. I had to pick up work at a visiting nurse association to meet the payments and my husband worked close to 60 or 70 hours a week. It was ridiculous — I wasn't seeing any of my kids or watching Geno's games.

The following summer, the VNA (Visiting Nurse Association) offered me twice the salary I was making, so I stopped working as a school nurse. I loved that job and wished I had it now; but I had to think of my family and the money I made at the VNA covered Geno's tuition.

Making that job change was huge — life was different and wonderful. I went to every one of Geno's games his sophomore year and also drove out to meet him at his campus every now and then.

He started to date Heather, whom he met in his freshman year. When I would ask him about them as a couple, he'd say, "Mom, we're too early in our relationship, I have no idea where it is going."

But Heather was a delight; somehow, she grounded my son and seemed to help make him feel good about himself. I hoped he realized what a gem of a girlfriend he had.

It seemed to me they got serious over the years. They had been going together a while when my Aunt Lillian died. She left her diamond engagement ring to me.

She told me if Geno and Heather married, she wanted them to have her diamond. "OK, Lil, but I am a little surprised," I told her. "I thought you would leave it to one of your nieces."

"Well, when I met Heather and saw them together, it reminded me of your uncle Frank and myself during our first years of dating." So, I promised her.

But I never got to tell Geno or Heather, as their relationship had ended because of his worsening addiction and I was afraid to even keep the ring in the house as his disease worsened after college.

Geno's hockey continued and so did the pain in his shoulder.

And, following along, so did his drug use to combat the shoulder pain. Somehow, he was able to obtain drugs on the street when he couldn't get a refill from his doctor.

He told me years later he popped a couple of Percocet right before each game and after each period so he could at least play reasonably well. I never really knew how much he was using; he didn't discuss it with me and even though I was a nurse I couldn't tell.

But it became apparent, though, that it wasn't just the physical pain he couldn't tolerate, it was the emotional issues as well.

One night he was on the ice and his shoulder popped out. I could see him go to the bench holding his arm, trying to push it back into the socket. Once again, his teammate helped him push it back into place. I was watching the whole scene from the stands and my husband was oblivious!

"Gary, his shoulder popped out!"

He replied, "No, Kate, he took himself off the ice because he was tired."

"Are you not seeing what I am seeing? His teammate is helping him shove his shoulder back into place."

"It's your imagination, I am watching the game, and look, he's back on the ice!"

I was furious. I was hoping this was the end of his career.

But, no, it went on like this for two more years with one knee surgery in his junior year that kept him off the ice for half the season.

CHAPTER 21

REFLECTION

I t came to me that athletes like Geno love the game so much they don't care about injuries or if it eventually kills them! Even if family, friends, girlfriends begged them to stop they wouldn't consider it. In my experience, anyway they just keep on keeping on no matter what.

All the time he continued to play he took pain medications, legal or illegal. I often wondered how he could endure the banging against the walls in hockey and the slamming around, the inevitable pushing around that was part of playing hockey and the tackles in football that eventually ruined his knees.

Geno told me he loved it; hockey was the true essence of what he was and he wouldn't stop, ever; but eventually he had to because his body could not tolerate any more.

One night his girlfriend Heather and her mom Deb came to a game of hockey. Thank God Geno didn't get hurt that night. Sitting with them I realized how much they, too, loved my son, and over the next few years before he graduated we got together for a dinner before Christmas.

I loved those times. Geno had let me back in his life. He had been so mad at me at times in high school and college about the abuse, he often disregarded my calls. And after his games he was quiet, wouldn't talk because of his anger and my insisting he stop playing hockey in college.

In hindsight, I should have left him alone as far as hockey went; but I would get frustrated and occasionally threaten to stop his college payments if he didn't get off the ice.

Gary didn't agree with me and I was the bad guy, according to Geno.

Seeing him in emotional and physical pain became too much for me and we would argue, always bringing up that he was sexually abused and needed the outlet of sports.

But as he grew up things changed. He forgave me but didn't or couldn't forget the family member who did this to him

.

CHAPTER 22

GENO, 20-SOMETHING

After Geno graduated from college with a degree in marketing, he got a job working at Molding and Millwork in Southboro. He was making a good salary, and after being there for about three years, he was promoted in the company. He was on the road. A company car that came with his own customers and territory.

I would have thought he would be happy at this point, but somehow, he didn't seem to be. I asked him directly one night when he came for dinner. He looked sad, discouraged and also a bit high on something, probably pot. I hated seeing any of my kids stoned, drunk or whatever so it bothered me that Geno would show up obviously under the influence.

"Roast beef dinner, Ma, *awesome!*"

He reached in the fridge for a cold one. We locked eyes.

"You're driving honey, and it looks like you've already had a few," I commented.

He rolled his eyes and flipped the beer open.

"I'm cool, Katie."

"I've got my eye on you, buddy."

We talked about his job as I made the gravy and got the mashed potatoes ready.

"If things are great with work, why do you look so sad? Is there something going on?"

He just looked at me and didn't say anything.

"You know me, Geno, I'm psychic," I said, trying to keep it light but looking for an answer from him.

He laughed at me.

"I'd rather you would just open up and tell me what's going on."

"Not now, Ma, can we just eat?"

I was quiet and almost gave up on the conversation but then I said,

"How is your relationship with Heather?"

Geno has been open with me most of our lives so it didn't come out of nowhere when I asked him his intentions with Heather.

"I love her — we really understand one another, but I think I love her more than she loves me.

After Geno died, I went out with Heather one night; she had been a big help in informing me about their relationship from beginning to the end.

When I told her Geno said that to me, she stated she thought it was the opposite; that she loved him more.

But at the time of my conversation with Geno I replied;

"Hey, you're only 26, you both need time."

"It's more than that. She is a good girl. She needs someone better than me, someone she can count on; we're different in some ways."

"Well you've been together for a long time, it seems like she loves you and I love her, you couldn't find anyone better than Heather."

Tears came to his eyes.

"Why don't you have a heart to heart with her and try living together."

But it was too late, Geno had rented an apartment above Breen's, a local bar in Worcester. I knew she would never consent to living above a bar nor did I blame her. I felt trouble and evidently Heather did as well. Geno moved in with one of his college friends.

He put on his coat, he was brushing me off and kissed me goodbye. I watched him take off down the street, stopping and talking with some of the neighbors he saw on the street. Geno always loved our neighbors, the kids he grew up with.

Maybe he should have stayed home until he found himself, I thought.

CHAPTER 23

WHAT'S GOING ON? 2015

I wasn't quite sure why I kept believing Geno when he told me his drug use ended, except for pot. Now I realize it was my own serious denial — I thought God wouldn't give me two sons with addictions. My son Dan started drinking in middle school and that is a whole different story and book, but he has been sober for more than 20 years. Sobriety: It was something Geno couldn't get a grip on.

Is obtaining sobriety with drugs different from alcohol? Personally, I believe so.

Heroin is the most powerful drug; only a small percentage of users can kick it.

I found out Geno was doing drugs seriously when his friend from Assumption college called us. He told us that he and Geno were both using Percocet. This friend had taken off to California to kick his habit and go to a rehabilitation facility there, but Geno owed him two thousand dollars and if he didn't get it he was going to take legal action.

We called Geno and told him to get home. He arrived, fessed up and we paid the kid the $2,000 dollars that Geno owed him.

My son looked all disheveled as well as sad. He cried and cried, just couldn't seem to get himself together.

He was a broken 27-year-old. My heart ached for him but we needed to be tough as well and Gary and I needed the truth.

He owed several people more money. We decided to help him out and paid the friends he owed; we had faith in him after a deep discussion about drug addiction we asked him if he needed a rehab.

He felt with Narcotic Anonymous meetings and keeping his job, he would be okay.

We gave in. It wasn't our first rodeo with addiction and we would give him a chance.

When I paid back his friends, I told them to never give Geno any more loans and if they did, it would be their responsibility if they lent him money.

But the worst, far more serious, was to come.

Geno had gotten a loan from his older brother Dan to open up a business. There was a lot of money involved; Dan was living out of the country. The plan was they would go into business together and flip houses or do some investing. Dan trusted him. The deal between them happened before we knew anything about the seriousness of his substance abuse, and the level it had taken him to. The transaction had already been made and it was between the two of them.

I guess Geno tried, but his disease became so severe, so horrible, that he ended up spending every bit of his brother's money on drugs.

Gary and I were furious. We had helped him out with owing his friends money, but he brought borrowing money from a loan shark to a whole different level.

When his brother Dan's money was gone, Geno started gambling to make the money back. But he lost at gambling and the loan shark he owed money to threatened to kill me and my adorable golden retriever, Frankie. He had found us on Facebook.

"What's this idiot's name, Geno?" I said angrily after he told me.

He gave me his name. I talked to a former police chief I knew and told him the story and gave him the name of the man who was threatening to murder us. He told us the guy would follow through with his threat.

"Kate, do you have the money?" He had a scared look on his face.

"I guess I can dip into my 401k."

"Do it. This is serious."

So, my husband, Gary, and I were off and running trying to fix Geno and get him back on track.

The night we found this all out, Gary went to Geno's apartment in Worcester; he wasn't there but Gary found him at the bar downstairs.

Our son was shaking, sipping on a beer he couldn't even pay for.

"I'm scared dad, Danny will kill me when he finds out all his money is gone."

"You're moving out of here Geno, give your notice and you're coming home."

We helped him clear out his apartment; he looked like a lost soul and truly believed his brother would kill him.

But first things first, we had to somehow get the money to the loan shark before anymore damage was done.

Thank God my husband is street smart and somehow squared it away. He never talked about it, and never will; some things Gary just keeps to himself. I knew his heart was broken. We didn't bring up our kids to end up like hoodlums.

But Geno was very sick, both physically and mentally.

Geno lost his job at Molding and Millwork. After many attempts to keep him there, his boss Justin just had to let him go.

He had gotten into a few accidents, one of them while driving under the influence.

When Geno died, Justin put on the card "Geno will always be a part of Molding and Millwork." That meant so much to Gary and me. He was truly loved there by Eric, his co-partner, and Justin and many others. My thanks to all of them for loving my son and trying to help him.

But Justin had to let him go for the good of the company and Geno understood.

"I screwed up, Mom. They knew I needed help and had to make me leave; Justin gave me about five chances."

One thing about Geno that I love to this day, he admitted when he was wrong. Guilty as charged.

He was sad he had to leave his apartment In Worcester, but I believe that's when his problems escalated. Living above a bar brings no good to anyone who has an addiction.

But they loved and cared about him. He continued to be "the man," as one of the guys told me as we packed up his clothes and furniture. He had to come home. Temporarily we hoped. Set some restrictions, make him go to Narcotics Anonymous meetings, even AA meetings although he didn't like to drink.

Geno hated all 12-step programs. He saw drug dealers he knew outside the NA meetings, waiting to attack the vulnerable that had to go to meetings in order to meet the requirements to live in a sober house.

"It's all a joke, Mom," he told me more than once.

I shook my head and thought I was too involved in this kid's life. Heather had long broken up with him and he was losing some friends. She stayed in touch with him and tried to help him; but she was probably as frustrated as Gary and I were. We all wondered when and how he would he pull himself together, if ever.

Geno was such a smart kid, a good friend, but this opioid addiction was killing him and his wonderful spirit.

My Al-Anon meetings helped. I got tough; Gary not so much. He wanted to deal with the situation in a different way. His idea was to love his son and let whatever he was going through run its course.

I didn't agree and I probably nagged too much.

But I had my own set of issues. Back surgery from my arthritis and foot surgery both involved lots of narcotics. I would discover my own medication would be missing. I guess I didn't hide it well enough.

Percocet was getting too expensive, at least 40 bucks a tablet on the street, so Geno moved on to heroin because it was cheaper.

During this time, he still tried to work and always found something. He sold Christmas trees one winter as well as the life insurance. But he couldn't kick his addiction.

He always hated needles; getting immunizations as a kid, he would grin and bear it. Evidently, years later, he learned how to inject the heroin and fentanyl. I felt hopeless and sad. I would look at his graduation picture from high school and college. He was so handsome with so much potential, but now he didn't seem to care. His main objective when he woke up every day was to get a fix.

As the heroin use continued and my son needed money to feed his addiction, he turned into a different person. He treated me as if I were the one with the addiction. If my money was missing he claimed I spent it, saying to stop blaming it on him.

He was starting to make me crazy. And, worst of all, I was starting to believe him.

Why?

Because addicts have a way of manipulating, lying, and treating people like they have the problem, not themselves.

Often Geno would give an excuse for not paying his friends back; I could hear his conversations and excuses they would extend the time of him paying them back. But he seldom did pay them back. He would ask us for money to pay his friends back. We would offer saying we would send them the money, but he didn't want it to work that way, he wanted the control, because in reality he was going to buy more drugs and had no intention of paying them back whatsoever!

Geno was still loved during his addiction because he was Geno. He always helped others if he could.

One day he and I were in a parking lot getting groceries. I looked around for him and Geno had put the groceries away and was changing an elderly woman's flat tire.

But his desperation for daily drugs led him to his self-destructive behavior and he would lie, cheat, steal, anything to make himself feel normal. He needed opioids to simply keep himself from not feeling dope sick. At some point, he wasn't even getting high, he just took them to maintain his physical and emotional state.

We tried. My brothers and sisters, friends and colleagues did their best, but Geno could only last for a couple of weeks and then relapse.

Of course, every time he got sober we would get our hopes up, only to be let down. He would leave the house in the morning to go to some kind of work he'd found, such as helping a neighbor with landscaping or painting a house- only to see him walk up the street at night swaying, talking to himself or to someone on the phone looking for more drugs.

My hopes would be shot; he was at it again.

This roller coaster of hope and despair wasn't totally new to me; it reminded me of my childhood. My dad was in and out of recovery from alcoholism. I never knew what to expect. My mother was typically laughing and cheerful, but when my dad drank the smile was gone, no more whistling.

In fifth grade, I was with my friends at the Five and Ten in Cushing Square in Belmont; we were walking out the door, heading home and I saw my mother exiting the bank. No smile. I knew my Dad was drinking again and for sure, he was; he'd lock himself in his bedroom with his whiskey bottle for days and sadness just lingered in the household until he was ready to sober up. Sometimes it was months, even years, he would stay sober, but I never knew when or if it was going to change.

***

Geno's behavior would get worse when he was high; he would yell and scream, wake everyone in the house up, cook and blast music at 3 in the morning, all the while thinking nothing was wrong with his behavior.

I got the guts to toss my son out several times, but the minute I said "detox" he would take off for days, with me having no idea if he was dead or alive. He eventually would show up at home and sneak in the den window. He would wear us down to the extent that we felt sorry for him, letting him sleep over and giving him a small amount of money.

This cycle of feeling sorry/giving in to him was especially hard during the holidays. Hoping for the best, we'd give him a break and let him be a part of the family and just try to hide money and credit cards if we knew he would be around. And if he joined us at a friend's house or one of my family members we'd have to warn them Geno was coming and to guard their cash and credit cards.

In the meantime, we continued looking for drug rehabs for him; he would tell us he wouldn't go and that he'd run away if we found one. We continued to put his name on waiting lists for detox centers and Suboxone clinics, which were also a three month wait. Suboxone is a drug that helps you to not use heroin; some insurances cover it, some don't. Treatment centers that take MassHealth, the free coverage for low-income residents are almost always full, especially during the winter.

An addict will steal, we knew that, or deal drugs to support their own habit, we knew that, too. If we just guarded our things could we all just enjoy him as the loving family member we always knew? He could be around his relatives, eating, talking, connecting with the cousins he grew up with. I was co-dependent, I watched everything he did. I knew I couldn't trust him but at the same time I wanted my familiar son back; the good kid we brought up. Perhaps I was sicker than he was at those times.

CHAPTER 24

REFLECTION, THANKSGIVING AFTER GENO

November came, the day before Thanksgiving 2016. Geno had been gone almost six months.

I woke up that morning feeling irritable, sad, lonesome, angry and couldn't figure out what to do with myself.

I was starting a new job in December and had to get a test for tuberculosis. On the way back I walked our dog Frankie around the Willards Woods conservation land in neighboring Lexington. I told Frankie we needed to talk to Geno, as if he really understood.

The year before the three of us had walked the same path and we had so much joy that day. Geno and I laughed, hugged, and watched Frankie play with the other dogs.

But this November 2016 was different. My heart ached so badly I didn't know what to do. I didn't know how I could stand it.

I cleaned the house that day and found the hat Geno gave me when he graduated from Assumption. I put it on as I swept the floor, and played music while I tried to figure out which of my friends to call to support me. But I decided to wait.

My family arrived around 2. Jessie was helping her Dad cook the turkey and my sisters brought dessert and drinks. I kept thinking of the Thanksgiving the previous year; I couldn't believe Geno was not here.

But this was a new chapter and his promise to stay sober the Thanksgiving before didn't happen. But this first holiday without him, I realized he couldn't get better; he lost faith in himself and didn't know how to get it back.

We all gave a toast to Geno in heaven and of course, my witty sister Denise said, "Well, at least he didn't have to see who won the presidential nomination!"

I talked to my sister Irene, an almost unbelievable story that I will talk about later, as she had a tumor and they gave her six months to live if she didn't get chemo. Still, she refused to accept because of her own beliefs about choosing medical treatment. That I did respect but I couldn't possibly lose another family member. Please, God, I prayed, I can handle some curveballs but not another one now.

I took Irene's positive energy and went out into my Woburn world, the neighborhood that was home for so long and tried to be open-minded as I would inevitably run into neighbors.

But the one neighbor I saw that day told me what I was going through was only the beginning. "The grief will be a lot worse at Christmas," she said.

Not true. I had been to my bereavement group the night before and the members of the group there seemed to be filled with hope. Geno was in heaven and they encouraged me to believe that.

I walked on and ran into the Clarkes, Geno's best friend Timmy and his mom Diane. They hugged me and told me everything would improve, and encouraged me to stay positive.

I looked at Timmy. He had some tears in his eyes but I told him to always remember Geno and move on and know that his friend would meet him in heaven, because he believes in eternal life. Timmy and Geno were great friends. He was what I would call a "true blue." Tim and his daughter stop over frequently, we are blessed to have him in our lives.

Tim is an amazing kid; he did the eulogy at Geno's Mass. That took courage. I believe someday he will be a public speaker — maybe Geno will help him, his guardian angel in heaven.

RESCUING/
DOING DAMAGE, 2015

A s I was told by Geno's probation officer in Westboro, "He's 29 years old — let go."

I didn't get a chance to tell her I had been going to Al-Anon, a companion/support group who have people in their lives whose substance use, either alcohol or drugs, affects and bothers them. Because I had family members affected by the disease I had been going to Al-Anon for 20 years and was aware of co-dependency, and the tools of the program: reliance on a higher power, letting go, tough love. How often I had heard "if you baby them you'll bury them."

I didn't want to bury my son, so I continued to go to as many Al-Anon meetings as I could and tried to convince my husband to come along. But he had his own way of dealing with Geno's illness, which seemed to be accepting his disease and praying he would get better; we were not on the same page; our marriage was starting to decline, something had to change.

Things reached a low when at one point all his narcotics were gone and Geno begged me to take him to Worcester to buy some more. He was getting sick. He now knew he needed a detoxification center then a rehab, but being on Massachusetts health, which is a free insurance there were never any free beds available for him. He called or I called detox facilities daily to see if there were any MassHealth beds; negative. The private rehab/detox hospitals were astronomically expensive, far beyond what we could afford.

I couldn't stand to see him sick. I called suboxone clinics but there was at least a two month wait. And there were problems with suboxone, too, though not quite as deadly as heroin.

I still couldn't stand to see him sick, so I gave in and drove him to Worcester to his dealer.

My money, my car. Yes, I was as sick as my son for doing this.

The following week I went to lunch with some close Al-Anon friends, Joanne and Laura. I had to confess about buying the narcotics. I felt so guilty, I had to tell someone. So, I told them what I'd done. Joanne looked me in the eye and said, "Seriously? You worked hard for that RN [registered nurse] after your name. The Worcester police probably have your car on radar, do you want to lose your nursing license if you're caught?"

"Never mind losing her nursing license, you could go to jail!" said Laura.

I pictured the series "Orange is the New Black" and knew I wouldn't risk being behind bars, the world knowing what I did and the feeling of the cell door locking and suffocation taking over.

The previous fall, Geno had court-ordered drug testing and meetings with his probation officer and things at home got somewhat better, so I thought.

He worked at different jobs; the local grocery store, selling life insurance. He had had several arrests and lost his license, so he always needed rides, depending on family members, friends to get him rides to where he needed to go until he got his license back.

I didn't know why he lost his license. Geno's life became vague to us — what he had done and what he was guilty of. Some of the crimes were when he was living in Worcester, he evidently got in a car accident that wasn't his fault, but the police had some suspicions and inspected the car, only to find drug paraphernalia. He hired his own lawyer and was put on probation.

His life was a rollercoaster ride; he was either on top of the world or heading down fast. He was not telling us about many of the crimes he committed and went about paying his fines. But when he moved back to our house he had to come clean in some respects. We found out he lost his license when a few days after Xmas of 2015 we had a snowstorm. Gary was sleeping as he had been working non-stop with the snow we had, or water breaks, whatever. He seemed relieved to get called into work to get away from our now labeled dysfunctional home.

I heard his work phone ring around 11 p.m. I assumed it was work. But no. I was sleeping on the sofa, Geno and had grabbed my keys to head down to the convenience store. He never made it, skidded into a car and totaled it right on our street. The phone call to Gary was Geno, he was walking up the street to get him so he could have an adult there when the police came. Unfortunately the police came before they made it back and Geno was charged with leaving the scene of a crime. Geno was sober, thank God, but leaving the scene of a crime was just as bad.

"What's wrong with him?" I screamed into the phone to one of my Al-Anon friends.

"Kate, honestly, why are you leaving keys around so he can just take off?"

And she was right. I knew from then on to hide every possession that mattered to me; often times this sick son of mine could manipulate, fool me, and treat me as the addict. I had Percocet around from my last surgery, so Geno frequently told me I was just as bad as he was, still using drugs when I didn't need them. I tried to explain to him that I also had pain and needed more surgery on my foot, he would tell me I was making excuses just like he did about his drug use.

He was somewhat correct—I was at my wit's end.

Gary and I couldn't tell when Geno was telling us the truth. We thought he still had his license but one night a policeman told us he was driving without a license and needed to take classes to get it back.

The strangest thing is, that I do not understand to this day, why the court system would have him take courses to get his license back. Legally he had to do it, he had no choice. I was told he had to prove he would follow all of the rules.

Then they would take his license away once again after getting it back, for another time, another incident that caused him to lose his license. And with each loss, he had to take a course to get his license back. Finally, he completed the program and was eligible to get his license to drive at the tune of $800, which we refused to pay.

I talked to his probation officer and told her we didn't want him to drive, he shouldn't be driving for the safety of himself and others. But once again it was one of the rules he had to follow. It just sounded like a big money maker to me.

"I have to do it, Mom, it is part of the rules or they will extend my probation."

"Then you need to work, pay your own way." But instead, he went to one of my sisters and borrowed the $800, went to the registry and got it back. I never knew when he had his license or didn't legally; even the law messed up. They said he would have his license suspended in another six months for another crime, but until then he could drive. Yippee!?

Now he would have another chance to get into another accident. It was so confusing but I didn't want him touching our car again.

None of this made sense to me, only that he had to follow rules he hadn't been following. But with his history, why would they let him get his driver's license back? Of course -money. Everything was about cash, the almighty greenback.

Every time he was called back to court for a continuation of some charge it cost him money or a fine; they didn't care that this kid was suffering with the disease of addiction. The judge would look at him and say,

"You owe $400, pay the cashier on your way out."

For what, I never knew. It was beginning to feel like a legal scam in the state of Massachusetts and when I tried to get an answer no one would return my calls.

It was insane. Geno told me to back off, it was Geno's life.

But really it was mine and my husband's, because he was living with us on and off and we had to deal with the difficulties he was causing.

Friends had suggested, "Just make him leave or drive him to the Pine Street Inn" a homeless shelter in Boston.

After trying that, several times, he would be back home. Sneaking in through the den window in the middle of the night, sometimes in good shape, others not so much. Often, he would be crying, trying to convince us he could get the old Geno back.

I was exhausted emotionally and physically. I gave in too easily and the family was in turmoil. Nothing helped: therapy, trying to get on the same page with my husband, listening to my social worker daughter's suggestions. I felt like giving up. I wanted to run away.

I finally confronted his two probation officers, wondering why they couldn't help get him into a program.

It's not our job to do that," I was told by Sandra McNabb, his probation officer in Westboro.

"What is your job, exactly?" I wanted to know.

My question was ignored.

Ashley, his probation officer in Woburn, explained she could help us section him.

"What does that mean?"

"If you feel he is unsafe to himself and others, we can place him into a facility."

"Where would he go?"

"Probably Bridgewater; a prison that is an hour or so south of here. It's really a good program."

"Really, Ashley? I thought it was a jail for sex-offenders — that is some of his problem, that he was abused."

"They are kept away from the sex offenders."

I told my husband that night. "We will find a solution, Geno's not going to Bridgewater" he said.

But we didn't get to discuss it with him because he called and said he was doing better and living with a friend in Lynn. He was starting his life insurance job again.

Through all of this, I thought Geno may have lost some brain cells with all the drugs, but he had passed the state exam to sell life insurance with flying colors. His boss had a lot of hope in him because he made close to $5,000 dollars the first week back on the job. He could be a determined money-maker kind of guy, and just as easily he could be sleeping on a park bench on Boston Common, penniless.

If he had a brain tumor someone would care. A doctor would order X-rays, CT scans, surgery if needed, some treatment plan, but addiction is a disease no one wants to recognize. The addict and whoever cares are the only ones who reach out. Shame, shame, shame on our legal and medical system, it isn't their place to get involved. So, whose place is it? In many cases the person overdoses and dies.

With any luck, there is someone who helps the person suffering with addiction, either through the legal system or a family member may loan money to get the addict into a recovery center. Until that happens the affected person is waiting for a bed to become available. If they continue doing drugs, they can overdose any time. I feared for my son's life every day.

I was supposed to have more surgery but I put it off. I was afraid to have drugs around or I wouldn't be available to help Geno if he needed me. Yes, some would call that co-dependency and enabling, others would call it love.

I admitted to myself that I just wasn't ready to take care of myself. I have severe rheumatoid arthritis, need two knee replacements and another foot surgery. So, I elected to wait and try all kinds of alternatives, vitamins, diet, and a drug called Enbrel as well as cortisone shots. I knew it was temporary but I wanted to get Geno better before myself. Does that sound like a woman who had been going to Al-Anon meetings for 20 years? Of course not, Geno was coming first.

CHAPTER 26

HOPEFUL AT HOLIDAYS, 2015

Christmastime 2015 came and Geno seemed to be getting better, not as volatile, no huge mood swings. Because his job was closer to our home we let him move back. We made out a contract with him, a suggestion from the therapist he finally went to. The rules, in order to live at home were going to Narcotics Anonymous meetings, helping around the house and working at his part-time job at a local grocery shop. And, if he could find rides with another co-worker, he would sell life insurance.

He also needed to give us his paychecks and his father would give him a small allowance. It was embarrassing for him but he knew he had to follow the rules in order to live here and get off probation.

He was getting clean urine test results which was a rule for probation. For me, there was the constant fear that my son would relapse. I tried not to worry, I handed his life over to God and prayed constantly. I called prayer lines, asked all my friends and family to pray for Geno, pray he would get sober and stay sober. I believed recovery could happen if he wanted it bad enough.

Our friends the Clarks came for Christmas Eve dinner with their adorable granddaughter Emma, and of course her dad, Tim. Geno was so good with her. He was good with every little kid—he loved them and they loved him right back.

"I could be a good father someday," Geno said happily.

In my head I could feel myself wanting to scream and say, "You need to get straight for good, you little A-hole."

But thank God it was only in my head. Instead the words came out a little kinder.

"You will be a great father someday."

And again, I prayed that it would come true.

But his sobriety didn't last. New Year's Eve, when we were on our way out, Geno came home stoned and we almost had to take him to the emergency room. But we sat with him and I explained we were now ready to call the police and have him sectioned, as he was a harm to himself and others; he heard the word "sectioned"; he left the house and we didn't hear from him for two weeks. He called from a friend's house and agreed to get help but "please" he said, "not Bridgewater." We told him to start looking for a facility and maybe we could find a bed available, somewhere, even out of state if his probation department would let him.

We thought about using some of our savings and sending him to California to a reputable" detox/rehab facility in the LA area; it was $50,000 for a month.

"What's the statistics of my son recovering for good?"

I asked a young man named Josh, before I dished out that much money.

"High success rate; over 80 percent," Josh said to me.

"Are you in recovery?" I asked.

"Yes, for four years."

"No alcohol, drugs of any sort?"

He hesitated.

"A few minor slips, but nothing for over six months."

"Good for you" I said to him, but not enough to convince me spending $50,000 and no guaranteed results."

The more stories I heard like this, the more I knew I had to detach from Geno — my heart was breaking but God was the only one who

GENO
THROUGH THE YEARS

Hockey years begin…1989-Geno

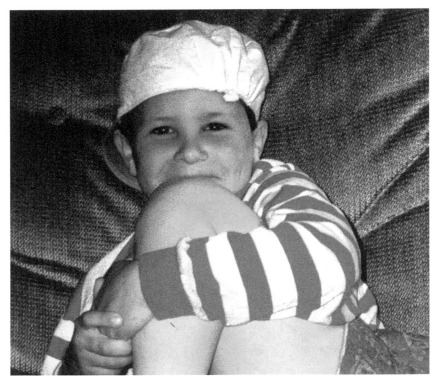

Geno at age 5.

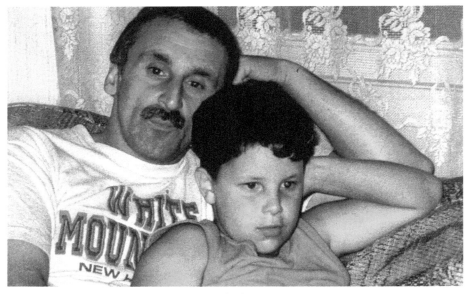

Geno and his dad, Gary, at age 5.

Geno at age 6, "Ripping one out of the field."

Geno's mother, Kate, and four-year-old Geno, 1989.

Geno and his cousin Casey, 1989.

Geno in our front yard in1990.

Geno playing "The Cowardly Lion" in the 5th grade play The Wizard of Oz.

Geno, third one from the left, with cousins Zack, Andy, and Johnnie.

Mom, Dad, and Geno in Maine, 1991.

Geno, third from the left, with cousins John, Zack, and Casey, putting on a performance for their grandmother.

Geno imitating his Dad at the "Highland Games," Sept. 1990.

Geno with his brother, Dan, and sister, Jessie.

Geno with Aunt Kerry and cousins Casey and Peter.

*8th gradeers Dan Surette and Geno at Central Park,
New York.*

Dinner out with siblings, parents, and a friend in 1999

*Neighborhood parents Karen Keane and Dan
and Diane Clark (Geno in background) in 1999
at his brother's graduation.*

*Geno, center, with Woburn buddies Tim Clark and
Kevin Keane, 2003.*

Geno, far right, with high school and college friends.

Geno, second from the left, with cousins Zack, Andrew, and John at Thanksgiving in 2000.

Mom Kate, and Geno at the junior prom at Governor's Academy.

Football game in high school.

Golfing with Uncle John at Eastman in New Hampshire.

Varsity Hockey in high school.

Woburn High School senior prom with friends.

Football team senior year, 2004. Geno is #4, marked by the blue circle.

Geno and his best high school friend,
Brian Gallagher.

Goodbye…be kind to one another.
The end of high school football.

Assumption friends Dan, Geno, and Phil, 2007.

Hockey at Assumption College. Geno is third from the right.

Geno's college graduation for "Hockey," 2009.

Geno lovin' the beach! 2010.

Geno and girlfriend Heather in college

"The Blues Brothers" — Cousin Peter, Andy, and Geno, 2014.

Geno with Auntie Carol and Uncle John, 2015.

Geno with the family dog, Frankie.

could intervene in my son's life to get him better; and maybe Gary and I needed to face the truth- there may be a low percentage of opioid recovery.

***

He had once again stayed with a friend, a wonderful kid he had been close to ever since college; Max Allen. They were roommates in college, on and off and one of the most loving and respectable kids I have ever met.

Max seemed to love my son like a brother, but his girlfriend not so much; and I couldn't blame her. They were starting their own relationship and didn't need an interfering kid disrupting their lives as they were trying to move forward.

I could tell Geno was feeling a big tumble in his life. He looked at Facebook too much and saw his friends in high school and college moving on. Some friends were making in the six figures, money means a lot to this generation. Plus, there were beautiful pictures with their girlfriends and trips they were taking.

I tried to tell him I was in the same position when I had my substance abuse issues in my early 20s. I didn't feel then as if I would ever get well. But I told Geno I learned to stop comparing myself to my friends and how well they were doing, their good jobs, cars, husbands. I was behind them in all circles.

"What happened?"

"I met your dad, and although we both had issues we worked on them together, left Massachusetts and went out west, had Jessie and the rest is history."

But my story didn't seem to matter; it was only some ammunition for him to use later on. He wanted an immediate do-over. He wanted to be 22 again, finishing college, having a good job with the potential of making a lot of money and a beautiful girlfriend who loved him.

Yet he gave it all up for the beautiful, yet short-lasting, feeling that shivered `through his veins, making him on top of the world until the high went. He had to look in the mirror eventually and would hate himself all over again until the next high made everything okay. Temporarily.

Time passed and neither of us could find him a bed for treatment in Massachusetts. Geno had asked his probation officers if he could go to Maryland as his friend from high school went to a recovery center there and had been sober quite a while; furthermore, Geno told them, he could get a job at his friend's company eventually.

The answer was an immediate no. While on probation he couldn't leave the state. He was discouraged.

Once again, he was able to get his license reinstated and he worked more selling insurance. He borrowed cars from friends or took public transportation to his clients' homes. The money he made was incredibly good but potentially dangerous to him because he would be tempted to misuse it. He asked his dad to hold it for him and Gary, once again, agreed to do so.

Geno showed up at our house one Sunday morning looking clean-shaven, suit on and ready to roll, as he put it.

"I am doing good, Katie"

I was washing the dishes listening to his jabba jabba. I had heard it before, but of course I hoped this time would be different. I wanted to see that Assumption College pride, the look in his eyes that said he could accomplish something; something other than copping dope from the worst sections of Chelsea, Worcester and also the most affluent areas of Newton.

Geno walked over and started drying the dishes. Since our dishwasher blew up right before the holidays he knew someone had to do it — he was the man of the hour.

I looked at him and he smiled. His beautiful teeth were chipping and the shades of yellow and lack of going to a dentist was evident. Poor nutrition, lack of regular dental hygiene, and the corrosive nature of whatever he was ingesting was showing up in his mouth.

"I know, my teeth, I promise Mom, I'll go back to being the old Geno, no drugs, I will permanently work and I'll get on a dental plan."

"You better, no girl of any substance wants a guy with yellow teeth."

He rolled his eyes at me but he knew we spent a lot of time making sure he went to the dentist. It wasn't the money going down the drain as much as we hated to see him like this; losing interest in what he looked like.

Boy, was I a bitch sometimes, but then again it was the mother in me. I knew, from going to 12 step programs, there should be no expectations.

"Mother, you have my word, pearly whites by the summer."

I knew his heart meant it but not so much in his drugged mind. I didn't trust him—how could I? As much as I wanted to believe it, my gut feeling, deep in my psyche, terrified me. I offered to ride to work with him.

"I'll go with you to your first [work] appointment today."

"God, Ma, you piss me off, can't you see I need to do this on my own?"

"Can't you see I want my son to live?"

"Please, I have to prove this to my boss. He is going on the appointment with me."

"Then why can't he give you a ride?"

"Mom, we've been over this. Would you like your patients see your mother drive you up to their house for a home visit with your old lady tagging along?"

I had to laugh at this. I pictured my mother sitting in the back seat when I was a visiting nurse, going through my medical bag, pulling out my stethoscope and try listening to her heart pounding, then she'd reach in the front and listen to my heart as I dodged cars because she was interfering.

Once again, I was unhappy he was allowed to get his license back.

He seemed sincere when he had called the day before asking to use the car. He had a client where there was no public transportation and it would be a big sale; the woman was a client in Concord, a well-to-do town west of Boston. She wanted to get a large policy for herself that would be left to her four kids; her husband had split two years before so she wanted to make sure her kids would be fine if something happened to her.

Geno was so believable. Either this was a big lie and he was a con artist or he was telling the truth. Somehow, I wanted to believe him....

I wiped my hands with a dish towel and handed him the keys.

"You need to call and update me; if Dad knew I gave you the car I would be in the doghouse."

The word "doghouse" reminded me of a cute story from my childhood, about how my friends the Murphy's had a jigsaw-cut wooden doghouse plaque on their kitchen wall. There were family members' names on individual wooden dogs to signify who was currently in trouble. Those were such interesting and fun times.

"Remember how they made a dog with your name on it and put it up there with the other family members? And you loved it when you were the one who was in the doghouse?"

"Wow, you remembered that story?"

"You told it to me about fifty time growing up!"

That was the trouble: There were too many cute stories from the past. The memories took me away from the harshness of what was really going on in the present but also the warm, beautiful stories of my connection with the Murphy's' growing up. Would I ever have grandchildren who I could tell these stories to?

"OK, enough. Go, go," I said as I handed over the keys.

"I love you Mom, you're the best."

"And the stupidest," I whispered to myself.

I was so weary, so tired that I gave in way too easily.

CHAPTER 27

SISTER IN NEED – JANUARY 2016

Irene was a true hippie — everything natural, organic and no preservatives. When the doctor mentioned chemotherapy, she promptly said no and continued with her probiotic diet and absolutely no sugar products.

Unfortunately, though, the tumor continued to grow and at that point she agreed to radiation therapy because it was too late for surgery.

Irene was calling to ask me if I could stay with her in Oregon during her treatment.

I couldn't get a flight fast enough. Going to the west coast, helping my sister, and getting away from my son would probably be the best thing for all of us.

Gary looked relieved when I told him I wanted to go. He helped me book my flight.

When Geno returned that night, I told him about my plan. Immediately he had one of his own in mind.

"Do I get to keep your car while you are gone?"

"I don't know," I told him. "How can I trust you for that amount of time?"

"Well it can't sit in the driveway being unused, that's stupid, look at all the sales I made just in the past 24 hours."

He tossed all the confirmed life insurance policies on our bed, more than $2,000 worth. Yes, my son was a hustler.

"Dad should hold on to those sales slips for you."

"Mom, once again, we have gone over this," he explained with elaborate—and mock — patience.

"My boss gets his percentage and he holds onto the slips. Then I get paid next week."

"I'm a stupido," I said to myself as I packed clothes, toiletries, toothbrush and several books into my backpack." I am too easy on you, you're really wearing me down." I heard Gary coming in so we filled him in about what had transpired in the last 12 hours.

"You still have two days to f-up, my friend." Gary looked at me discouraged and always concerned that I could never find something positive in this situation.

"How about positive thinking?" Gary commented. He had to get his say in.

"Dad, Mom, the car?"

Gary and I looked at each other. We both knew how Gary loved to stick me with the decisions. When I had told him a few days before that he got his license back until May he was equally as upset as I.

"We still shouldn't let him use it, Kate."

"I know, but he nagged me so much I let him use it for an appointment in Concord and it turned out OK; I'm sorry I didn't tell you about it."

"Why didn't you call me Kate? This is how fights start and our marriage will be affected."

"You are right, I won't do this again."

Geno came in the room and Gary wanted the control back.

"Mom told me she let you use the car."

"Yes Dad, but it worked out okay."

"Geno, you know the history of money when you get it, never mind the accidents" Gary said.

Gary looked at Geno seriously and said,

"In your hand for a minute, you make a few calls and that commission will end up in one of those great veins in your arm, or you will be buying Percocet's to hold you over."

Geno sat on our bed and cried.

"Please, one chance. Dad. If I screw up, the car goes and I'll go to rehab, deal Mom?"

"If you live to enter a rehab or if we ever find one that will take you!"

"It won't happen, I swear Katie, it just won't, I got the money bug back in me, I'm on a roll."

"I'll be in Oregon, it's going to be up to your dad and you—Geno, you will be one sorry dude if you do one thing wrong. Dad doesn't get mad often but when he does …well, you don't want to be there and your dad, well, gentle to a point but then he explodes, and I wouldn't blame him."

"I won't disappoint you, either of you. The crocodile tears were streaming down his cheeks, he really thought in his heart he could succeed. " I promise I'll try, I give you my word."

I blocked out some promises I made to my parents myself back in the day. I should have known better, because I was selfish and just thinking of my needs. Would Geno do the same? Or could he have an epiphany while I was away?

I left for Oregon two days later. Geno drove me to Logan Airport in Boston and gave me a bear hug.

"Love you Mom, I don't know why I did what I did in the past, but this is a new beginning for me."

"Just stay out of Worcester, that's where the trouble started."

"That's where you think it started Mom; when I got my first dose of anesthesia back in the ninth grade for my knee surgery, when I tore the meniscus—I fell in love with the stuff."

I think I had to agree with him on that one.

I walked away, heading into the area to have my luggage checked. He waved goodbye. To me, he looked 9 instead of 29. He was a child in a man's body.

"Get the anger out of your heart, don't feed the wolf," I called out to him.

There was a saying I hung in the computer room where all my kids did their homework. "Two Wolves." It was written like this, all in capital letters:

> "A NATIVE AMERICAN GRANDFATHER WAS TALKING TO HIS GRANDSON ABOUT THE TRAGEDY. HE SAID "I FEEL AS IF I HAVE TWO WOLVES FIGHTING IN MY HEART. ONE WOLF IS THE VENGEFUL, ANGRY, VIOLENT ONE, THE OTHER WOLF IS THE LOVING COMPASSIONATE ONE.
>
> THE GRANDSON ASKED HIM, "WHICH WOLF WILL WIN THE FIGHT IN YOUR HEART?
>
> THE GRANDFATHER SAID, "THE ONE I FEED."

I know my kids read that saying from time to time. I noticed them staring at it on the wall after they had an argument with someone, or even got physical.

"Where did you get that saying Mom?" my older son Dan asked one day years ago when he had a particularly bad day in high school.

"Auntie Renie sent it to me, she loves the Native American culture and she saw this one at an Indian reservation she went to in Arizona. In other words, Dan, anger will ruin your heart and you will get angrier and angrier about an issue, instead of just trying to let it go. Anger can kill your soul; love and forgiveness heals the heart and soul."

I tucked the saying in each of my kids' suitcases when they went off to college. I hoped it would help.

God wasn't giving me any clue as to what would happen next. The only instinct I had was to pray. So that's what I did as I got on the plane.

I pulled my late Aunt Lillian's rosary beads out of my carry-on. Before she died she told me I could have the beads that had been on her kitchen table for my entire life. Oh, Aunt Lillian. God, did that woman love Geno. They were born on the same day and he looked like her first boyfriend. No wonder he was her favorite.

As the plane took off, I thought of good ol' Lil, I guess I thought she didn't like me because I was not a good Catholic like the rest of my cousins but she loved my kids. As I prayed the first few beads of the joyful mysteries, I asked her to save my son, or ask Jesus to save him. I knew Geno could get into a heap of trouble on this planet earth, especially if I wasn't there to monitor.

But, boy, did I learn a lesson: My ego was just too large at times. I could play God easily and make his addiction cease. But there were hard life lessons I needed to learn: Only God was in control, I had to climb down from the higher place I was on and learn to turn my life and Geno's over to God.

As the plane headed to Oregon I thought about the hard work ahead of me with my sister and her friends. I wanted her to live, give radiation a try, but her friends there who believed in alternative medicine thought she should go natural — vitamins, minerals, all organic. They sounded like good people who loved Irene, but on the other side I felt they were bullies.

Time would tell. I was a nurse with the belief that Eastern medicine works but why take the chance of only vitamins to kill the cancer cells. I told her she should do both — radiation and the alternative meds she used.

The plane was ascending as I put the rosary beads in my pocket. I was so tired dealing with the last few months that a nap would do me good. I closed my eyes, faintly hearing the stewardess give instructions.

CHAPTER 28

WEST COAST MEDICINE

I landed in Medford, Oregon, and was picked up by my sister and her friend Gwen who would drive us to Ashland where Irene lived.

Renie looked worn, too skinny and, predictably, not as pretty as she used to be. She was pale, sad and broken. I could tell she couldn't wait to go home to lie down in her own bed

This wasn't the sister I grew up with. She was so exhausted, certainly not the sister who wanted to find a club to go dancing on most nights of the week. She moved over in the back seat to make room for me and I could see it then in her beautiful brown eyes. There was no hope, she was going to move on to heaven this year. I looked at her and gave her a smooch.

"I'm dying, Kitten."

"No such thing. You're moving from grammar school to junior high, a transition."

She hugged my hand harder and laughed.

"You still have your great sense of humor, even though you're going through so much with Geno!

I thought about the bubbly teenager who followed me around with my boyfriends, making sure I didn't have sex at 16. She would lecture me and my high school friends not to be intimate: No getting felt up, no third base, no sex!

"Not even first base, Renie?" my best girlfriend asked.

A loud "NO!" she'd shout, and my longtime boyfriend would leave, sneaking out the cellar door along with the other guys and my girl-friends. She could be a tough cookie. Later on I realized she didn't want me to repeat her life.

Irene herself ended up pregnant at the age of 18 when her boyfriend was home on leave from an army tour in Vietnam. She didn't want any-thing to interfere with my dreams of becoming a nurse.

I loved her husband Paul. He was a well-built kid. His nickname was "Tiger," possibly because he looked like a tiger but it may have been more because he could fight like one, too.

Paul had been a savior in my life and boosted my self-esteem when mine was in the gutter. He came into my life when I was fifteen. He loved me as a future sister-in-law and couldn't stand the guys I was putting up with.

I didn't know they were treating me badly but Paul did, and he guarded me like a father when a couple of them were around.

Paul would tell me to get rid of boyfriends who he felt were not wor-thy of me. God, I loved Paul, to this day I remember how he was the keeper of people that felt like shit. Somehow he couldn't help himself out of that same feeling, the low self-esteem. Dodging bullets in Vietnam can do that to you.

These memories were going on in my head as I was traveling to Ore-gon and I was telling Irene the stories I remembered later as we were relaxing and watching the news.

"I so loved my little nephew, Irene." Paul Jr. was such a cute little redhead. I felt like he was my kid as I changed his diapers and fed him his bottle.

"Paul's own father died when he was 33; he couldn't take the two tours of duty in Vietnam. He was never the same, arriving home with his own set of demons.

Paul's son, Paul Jr, had died of congestive heart failure, a result of a drug addiction, at the age of 39. He had followed in his father's footsteps but he seemed to relapse after his wife Aimee left him in the early 2000s.

"Now it might be my turn, Katie, I might join them if this radiation doesn't work."

I was angry and sarcastic. I was mad at her and her smart yet uninformed friends; talking her into rejecting the medical protocol for treatment of lung cancer.

Irene actually hated the medical establishment and the AMA (American Medical Association) guidelines. She never trusted them, she thought they were moneymakers and they didn't believe in alternative medicine. That last part was true in my experience as a nurse.

What would I do if I were in Irene's situation?

I thought about it and quickly came to what I would do for treatment. I would hop on the bandwagon of surgery but also beef up on vitamins and diet. No way would I feel comfortable using alternative medicine alone. I was open about my opinion on Irene's treatment back at home in Woburn.

"That's what Auntie wants," Geno had said in his quiet concerned voice once before I flew to Oregon. He was listening in on my conversation with another nurse friend of mine; I trusted Barbara's opinion.

I couldn't believe this was my child who was strung out on drugs dare have an opinion; as if he had no rights to express himself unless he stayed sober. I pretty much said those exact words to him.

He looked at me with fury.

"Because I am human with feelings and love Auntie! That was awful, Mom. You can be so heartless at times when it comes to what I have been and am going through. Just remember I have a heart, a good one, and even though I can't seem to like myself I love others, especially Renie and what she is going through!"

He tossed a washcloth at me, really furious.

"Think of that, Ms. Princess, maybe Irene just wants to die the way she wants to, and maybe I want to die because I don't feel like trying anymore. Ma, it hurts to live in this drug-addict world I got myself into and it's probably just as hard for Auntie to make the right decision. Either way, one of them will kill her; the cancer or the radiation."

I watched him run up the stairs and heard his door slam loudly.

Wow. My son cuts to the chase pretty harshly; does he really want to die?

But 20 minutes later he was heading out the door for a run with Frankie.

Geno ruffled his beautiful pale white-gold fur and I looked at my son enthusiastically. Geno was his best friend.

I watched the two of them run down the street. Yes, I can be an asshole sometimes. "Count to 10," my father use to say. "When you're angry, start counting, then usually the verbal diarrhea doesn't come out because you've had the time to think."

When Geno came back I handed him a facecloth, he was perspiring and I also needed to make amends.

"I am sorry," I said and reached over and hugged him. "I can be a real 'dick' sometimes, Geno."

I told that to my sister.

"I never knew Geno loved me so much," Irene said.

"Geno loves everyone in the family except me at this point," I said.

Irene wanted to know how Gary and Jessie felt about me leaving and helping her.

"Well, Gary wasn't thrilled I was going 3,000 miles away. He was scared and wanted me home. I could tell he didn't want to be babysitting his 29-year-old drug addict son alone. Sometimes, though, sometimes he seemed relieved, like I could be the problem. Geno and I were always battling and Gary was always breaking up our verbal fights.

Renie listened intently.

"The night before I left, Gary was grilling steak outdoors in 20 degree weather. I think being the cook of the family gets rid of stress.

There was a bit of snow coming down and I put my arms around his waist and leaned up to kiss him. I felt his tears.

"Wow, I'll be back you know! Or are you worried I might not, that I might find a cowboy that will sweep me off my feet."

Renie laughed at that.

"Not too many cowboys in Oregon."

"I love him Irene, but with all this going on I feel I might lose him unless things change."

"I doubt that, Kate, you and Gary have the best relationship in the family."

"He can only take so much; he's getting weary."

"Now I feel bad dragging you out here."

"I offered and I feel blessed to help you; sometimes being away from someone can actually bring you closer. I heard Robert De Niro say that in some movie, or was it Al Pacino?"

"Who cares, Kate, both of them are hunks."

We laughed.

"Tell me about your flight before I hit the sack."

I got out some lotion that I use in my Reiki practice.

"It was really a hoot!"

"So many thoughts were going through my head as I was sitting in between an older woman on my left and a 20 something boy on my right on the plane; the trip was taking forever and I hated being stuck in the middle. But I felt lucky to get a seat at all, the plane was full.

I asked the lady on the aisle seat if she would switch with me. "I have this bladder issue," I told her. "Would you mind switching?"

"Look at me, I'm 80 years old and 50 pounds overweight, you think I don't have a problem?"

Renie laughed hysterically, knowing my weak bladder, not holding much since junior high and on top of it I was claustrophobic, stuck in the middle and the college student needed the window seat.

The lady next to me kept tipping over on me and drooling; I nudged her numerous times and she'd look at me with her bloodshot eyes and apologize, she was definitely drinking.

"I really wanted a Valium so bad along with a glass of wine," I told Irene.

"Your downfall, kiddo," she said.

"Well I know that better than anyone, Sister."

I started laughing; "What's so funny?

"Mr. Harvard, the kid next to me, heard me mumble it and I guess he thought I was cool after all, so he started up a conversation."

"Do tell," Renie said as she pushed my hand over to rub her back, her right side where the tumor was, anxious to hear the rest of the story.

I asked "You live in Oregon?"

"I did but I go to Harvard now, just back to see my mom."

"An Ivy Leaguer, huh?"

He looked at me, "You familiar with Harvard?"

"My dad went there, we use to go to the reunions but mostly I hung around in the square through high school and actually through my 20s."

"Did you tell him how much dope we smoked in Harvard Square in that old cemetery?

"I think he figured that one out!"

We laughed.

"He asked me if I was a Harvard graduate, but I disappointed him in telling him Harvard didn't have a nursing school then."

I burst out laughing. "I was not really Harvard material anyway, but I am a nurse."

He seemed impressed until I told him I went to a hospital school.

The conversation came to an end. I guess he needed to talk to someone with a degree.

My friend with the big bladder and wouldn't switch seats snored and drooled twice more on me. I had to practically sit on her lap to get by her. It was humiliating for her."

The stewardesses had quite a laugh, as I did.

"Suddenly, Mr. Harvard asked me to name my favorite Shakespeare play. I decided to blow his mind so he would leave me alone.

"I have no idea, "I told him. "I was too drunk to remember anything, plus it was at the Shakespeare Festival, right here in Ashland, Oregon. It was the first time I took LSD and I tried to dance my way to the stage."

"I was with you and Gary, that didn't happen, or did it?"

"No, of course not, I was beyond those days but I felt like entertaining this Ivy Leaguer."

"The only time I took acid was a mistake. I was in nursing school, maybe 1971; my friends and I went to a party at Brandeis in Waltham. This guy was trying to hit on me and offered me a glass of something that was in a punch bowl. It had LSD in it and my friends were so scared they took me back to my dorm at Beth Israel Hospital and kept making me drink water. Finally, one of my nursing school buddies took me over to the Emergency Room because I was hallucinating. I was given a shot of something and they pumped liquids in to me the rest of the night. The hospital police made me report it to the school; that was the end of it but the whole thing frightened me enough that I never did hallucinogens again!

"Did Mr. Harvard get a kick out of your stories?"

"No that was it for the rest of the trip until he pointed out to me I wouldn't get proper photos from the airplane window. Thinking of you I gave him a loving look. You, Irene, would say, 'Love your enemy.'"

I finally got off the plane. It took 30 minutes for everyone to grab their luggage from the overhead bins. This was the final straw, Mr. Harvard trying to push past me to get his luggage above the bin when a large piece fell on Bladder Lady's head as she was still sleeping and drooling on the floor!

"OMG," Renie said, trying not to laugh but just the visual of it put her into hysterics. "Was she okay?"

Two attendants got a wheelchair and brought her out to where two EMTs were waiting; I did hear she was OK, but Mr. Harvard took off like a bat out of hell!"

"Dad used that expression, 'bat out of hell.'"

"I know, it just came to me now but that was a saying of Dad's."

"I am so happy to see you, Irene." I didn't mention how sad it made me to see her looking so sickly with her big woolly blanket and huge hat covering her head to combat her shivers.

I hesitated as I placed my hands on her forehead, the last part of the treatment I do with Reiki.

"I have to tell you I'm not crazy about your friend Gwen, Irene. She's bossy to you, and when I asked her to stop for coffee she seemed put out."

"She likes to make organic coffee at my house."

Irene was clearly getting sleepy, but was sticking up for Gwen; it was her girlfriend and her house, but I needed a good hit of Java to help me stay awake! But I got my wish, still I could tell Gwen hated giving in to me.

Pretty soon Rene was drifting off. I put her favorite woolly shawl over her; it was 11 p.m. West Coast time; she stirred, smiled at me but I could see her wincing.

"How's the pain, Irene?"

"A bit in my back."

"On a scale of 1 to 10, ten being the worst?"

"A nine."

"Two Percocet's now and one Oxycontin for you if you wake-up with pain my dear. That will get you through until the morning."

I put a warm pack on her back and we prayed together; my family of origin always relies on prayers when we are together.

Irene is usually the queen bee of praying, but she was too groggy tonight.

I honestly could feel my mother around us, her presence as we went through the glorious mysteries of the rosary. It felt so calming and healing.

I kissed Renie's forehead and set the alarm for 7:30 the next morning. We needed to be at her radiation appointment by 9.

All the instructions of Irene's day-to-day events were written down for me by her nurse friend Doreen, who included all the medications, time to take them, and her break-through pain medicine, Oxycontin.

I headed to the kitchen and poured myself a glass of wine to settle down and sleep; I often asked myself if it was a ritual or if my brain-body connection needed the alcohol. This trip wasn't a time to evaluate my alcohol use.

I was close to 3,000 miles away and I was scared my son would die without me there to monitor. What I learned was that he could die with me there. But it took me months to realize that. I thought I was his saving grace. Boy, would I need several Al-Anon meetings in a row for 20 more years to realize I wasn't in charge!

Geno could easily overdose on a park bench or in his bedroom with me around; I offered the rosary up that night for my strength in my belief of a higher power and for Irene, that the radiation would heal and she would have many more good years.

My sister woke up and burst into conversation about breakfast, what she wanted, where everything was and then proceeded to tell me the rules of the house!

"Rules? Since when does my hippie sister have rules?"

"I've changed a bit."

"Please don't tell me I can't have wine at night, I'll leave right now."

She laughed and opened the fridge — there stood four bottles of my favorite Chardonnay!

"You remembered! Soldiers, all standing in a row."

"I lived with you, how could I forget your wine, cheese and crackers every single night?"

"I didn't know you had any, I found one little 4 ounce bottle in my suitcase for last night, but thanks Renie Beanie. Whatta I owe you?"

"Seriously? Your life! You're alive because of me, Kitten."

"Oh, good one, Renie, thanks for reminding me!"

If nothing else on this trip, we had one good laugh after another.

I have to tell the story about my sister Irene's birthday: My mom was pregnant with her, due in mid-July of that year, and was sick of being pregnant, so she asked her doctor in Portland, Maine, to induce her so she could have a fourth of July baby. Who would actually request that?

My mom did just that, and the doctor went along with it. He gave my Mom general anesthesia on July 4th and 20 minutes later, Irene Isobel Carver came into this world with a bang. She has acted like a firecracker ever since: full of life, vibrancy and good, down-to-your-soul energy.

We didn't need to discuss how she saved my life because now it didn't matter. I am here and living the life God chose for me which includes him, but at the age of 22 I just didn't care much about living.

I had been sexually assaulted coming out of a bar in Brighton and life just didn't seem important until Gary came along and gave me the will to live. Between Gary and Irene I got my juju back and have loved life ever since; even with the emotional rollercoaster rides, tornadoes and hurricanes that hit my family. I realized it was still a beautiful world.

I had an epiphany when I was 50 that I have never forgotten.

That year Gary and I had been going through a lot of emotional turmoil with family that seemed too much to bear. I took a nap around 4 one afternoon after dropping Geno off for hockey practice. I had a beautiful dream, where God showed me life would be worth living.

I woke up to the sounds of birds, kids playing, laughing in the neighborhood and a feeling of total contentment washed through my soul.

I felt whole and beautiful inside and out, the angels were protecting me and God was telling me to never give up hope. I believed God was there for the long haul with me, whatever happened he had my back.

The day did look different to me. Geno had his high school friends over and they were playing whiffle ball in our back yard. Bases were set up years ago and they just played like boys; rolling on the ground, wrestling, arguing weather someone made first base or was out. I had the awareness of happiness, fun and beauty. I believed life from then on was going to be awesome, or I would try to make it be.

Irene looked at me, knowing I was in a reverie thinking about that life-changing dream way back when.

She shook me out of it, telling me another friend had arrived to help.

"Katie, Doreen is here, she is going to go to radiation with us so you won't bealone on the first day."

CHAPTER 29

INCARCERATION, JANUARY 2016

Doreen and I hit it off right away. Unlike Gwen, she turned out to be a sweetheart, just the person you would want taking care of you if you were hospitalized. She was smart, efficient and loved seeing people heal.

Doreen was devoted to getting Irene well. Her pretty green eyes would light up when the doctor explained to us, mostly me because I had just arrived, Irene's plan of care. I felt sad that she didn't have the surgery immediately because the tumor had been small enough to be removed when it was discovered. My sister didn't tell any of us back home how sick she was; we only found out because when we called her horrible hacking cough into the phone gave her away. It had gone on too long. Finally she confessed how bad it was, but refused surgery saying she preferred to deal with it "naturally."

As I mentioned before, she was being bullied into more of a homeopathic way of dealing with the tumor. I was so glad she reached out to me and we both hoped I could be of some help.

I was there for 10 days, trying to nurse my sister back to health when the phone rang around 10 pm Pacific Time.

My husband's name lit up on my iPhone.

"Something's wrong, it's 1 in the morning in Boston," I said to Irene.

But it was my daughter using Gary's phone- *oh no, is something wrong with my husband?*

"Hello, Mom. It's Jess."

She was crying but trying to keep a stiff upper lip.

"What's wrong, Jess?"

"Geno is in jail."

OMG, I said to myself, *at least he is not dead.*

I put the phone on speaker so my sister could hear.

"Is Dad okay, sweetie?"

"Neither of us is okay."

She sounded tired and angry and I couldn't blame her.

I wished they had waited until the morning, now I would be up all night worrying. Jail was the place with murderers and pedophiles. I remember Geno telling me how claustrophobic he was and visualizing him locked in a cell, all alone frightened me.

I thought he might hang himself or slit his wrists

These thoughts went through my head in a matter of seconds.

Irene gave me the signal to ask how Gary and Jess were and what had happened to put him in the clink!

"He was allowed to make one phone call, he called Dad and told him he had worked at the insurance company but later went to Worcester to see friends; they picked him up for speeding and the police found drug paraphernalia. That's where dad is now, getting the car. It was towed to someplace in Worcester. Dad wanted the car home, he's going to court tomorrow morning in Westboro."

"They wouldn't let Dad bail him out?"

"Mom, think about this; he's speeding, high on drugs and you really want Dad to bail him out?"

"I can't stand the thought of him locked up, Jess! Couldn't they release him to a detox or whatever? I don't know, I'm scared for him."

I could feel her frustration with me; she kept telling me to get tougher and get to more Al-Anon meetings. As a social worker, she knew what the right answer was, keep him safe, and if jail would keep him safe, so be it.

"I would have waited to call you in the morning but dad needs the credit card/debit number. The one he has isn't working- just in case they let him out tomorrow."

I went to my purse and gave her two of my credit card numbers, she was tired and she promised to call tomorrow.

Irene was sitting in the rocking chair that she inherited from my mom when she died. My mother use to rock my kids to sleep in that chair. She would be so sad if she knew what was going on with her grandson.

I walked over to Renie. She had poured me a glass of wine. I drank the 6 ounces in two big gulps. She looked at me and laughed.

"No worries, Sista, it's not 1972, you won't see me guzzling wine again while I am here."

"I've heard that before." She was joking and I wasn't.

"NO GUZZLING, I ASSURE YOU!" I yelled it.

I sat by the rocking chair , almost howling like some kind of animal you might hear in the night.

Renie patted my head, "It will work out Katie, God won't let him die, not now anyway."

"How do you know?"

"Because I need you here, and Kate, Geno is very sick, maybe jail will do him good."

"But he has been good for a month now; if he is getting high I don't know how he is getting away with it because his drug testing has been clean."

Renie was rocking gently, I knew she was ruminating, wanting to tell me something but hesitating.

"Spit it out, Sis."

"Have you heard of a whizzinator?"

"A what?"

She laughed. "It's some kind of contraption, a fake penis that a guy can fill with urine, shove it in his pants and when he is tested with a monitor in the room the guy producing the urine sample can get away with it. It looks very natural, but he can fill it with someone else's urine ahead of time and the drug screen comes out clean."

"My God Irene, this seems very far-fetched," I said, and I burst out laughing.

"So, you think Geno owns one of these and fools the monitors when he's tested?" I had to ask her.

"It's a good possibility, someone in AA told me his son who is an addict purchased one on Amazon."

Even though I was worried and upset, even sad, this story made me laugh and realize I had to face reality about my son. He could have been fooling everyone, with or without a whizzinator.

I had certainly been in denial, I knew that.

Irene and I stayed up most of the night; we were too nervous to sleep.

"You need some shut-eye, Renie, I should be helping you and it's the other way around!"

I looked at my watch "It's five in the morning. Let's try to sleep for three hours and then we'll both nap after radiation this afternoon."

Irene offered me a Percocet; she had over 100 tablets, her pain was that bad and my arthritis was flaring.

"No, kiddo, Motrin is fine."

I tucked her in bed and went for a walk; the birds were waking up as well as the milkmen. "Milkmen?" Wow, I haven't seen one of those trucks since the late '50s, but here in Ashland there were quite a few.

I remembered my milkman Fred who showed up weekly and left about 10 gallons. My two brothers drank most of it to wash down their peanut butter and jelly sandwiches. My mind must have been searching for any kind of distraction—why was I thinking of milk, milkmen and the 1950s?

It was early west coast time. Gary and Geno would be in court now. The outcome was up to the judge. He had tried to get in touch with his lawyer without success so he was relying on a public defender. Jess had told me Gary was going to try and get him into a medical facility rather than staying in jail.

While Irene was getting her radiation, Gary called. He was hoping to pay bail and had discussed with the public defender about getting Geno into a detox, but the judge refused. The court was insisting on punishment for him.

I had talked to his probation officer before, many times, she was a tough cookie. Later in the day I called her, pleading with her to let my son get the medical help he needed. But it wasn't their job, someone had told me this before, either in Woburn or Westboro. I was getting mixed up. Regardless, it was only their job to either fine him more money for each offense or put him in jail or section him if he was in harm's way. That's exactly how it was put to me.

They felt they had given Geno too many chances; he had to stay in jail for a month until his hearing.

"My God, isn't addiction an illness?" I screamed at his probation officer. "Can't you get him a bed in a detox or rehab I shouted over the phone? Would you stick a cancer patient in a drug rehab?"

I was so furious and was losing my temper. Irene mouthed the words to get off the phone!

But I had one last thing to say: "Are you a mother?"

No answer.

"Well, if you are, would you insist your kid get real help or go to jail?"

Her silence was infuriating, so I hung up, mainly because the probation officer wasn't paying a bit of attention to me. She had probably turned me right off, may have even skipped out to the bathroom and was laughing at me while sitting in the stall.

I had intended to stay a month in Oregon until Irene's radiation was over. I was now at a loss as to what to do. Gary wanted me home, Irene needed me there.

I talked to her friends about it. Doreen was more than willing to take over my sister's care but her other two close friends felt like she needed family. God would give me some kind of answer.

Irene started to get nauseous from the radiation. She was given Compazine, a drug that seemed to work. Her friend Gwen was so upset about administering this medicine that while I was out grocery shopping she gave Irene sauerkraut for the nausea. Evidently that sauerkraut was an alternative remedy for nausea in cancer patients.

My German grandmother would have been mad at me for tossing out the sauerkraut and told Gwen not to visit Irene when I was here. As much as I believe in all different cures I felt that wasn't one of them, or one I believed in, anyway.

Geno was in jail. I ended up staying longer to help Irene.

A week after I got there, Rene started to improve. She was eating better and even put on some much-needed weight.

I made a reservation to Boston on United Airlines.

Geno called me from the jail every day. Jessie somehow knew how to put money in an account for him. We could talk briefly but he made it clear not to mention what happened. Everything was being recorded, so I kept my mouth shut. His court date was set for February 22.

So I still had some time left with Renie.

CHAPTER 30

RETURNING FROM OREGON

I arrived home from my sister's on February 12. Gary hugged me hard at the baggage claim; he had tears in his eyes.

"Thank God you're home, I couldn't take care of Frankie alone."

Frankie, our golden retriever?

I hugged him.

"We'll be okay, Frankie will be okay," I said.

But I wanted to say, if that was the issue we could have gotten a friend to watch him.

But I kept quiet, I knew there was more to it than that.

While I was still in Ashland, Gary and I had talked about getting a lawyer instead of using a public defender. We needed someone who took my son's illness seriously and could get him into a rehabilitation facility.

Jessie had researched criminal defense lawyers while I was out there and she came up with a few.

We decided on a Boston firm, which turned out to be a mistake. He had thought he could get Geno into a rehab easily because he knew the district attorney in Westboro, as he worked with her in the past.

My sister Kerry and I were skeptical and we searched every rehab in Massachusetts and they were all full. The waiting list was two to four months.

His probation officer wanted him to stay in jail for six months. Our lawyer said if we found a rehab he could convince her and the judge to let him enter a facility that would deal with his addiction.

The only place we could find was a rehab in Florida that my sister Kerry mentioned to us. Kerry is a drug and alcohol addiction counselor and she knew that this was a good place, as it was a working facility. Once they were approved to work, after so many weeks, the staff would help them find a job and the client could pay room and board and continue to get counseling.

On February 22 Geno stood before the judge. The lawyer presented his case, explaining that this rehab in Florida had a good success rate for addicts and that was his recommendation since there were no beds/rooms available in Massachusetts or any other nearby states.

The judge laughed at him, threw the paperwork on the floor and refused to let Geno leave Massachusetts.

The judge's laughter didn't last. "I'd like to be in Florida myself." He was actually screaming at Geno.

The lawyer said nothing, didn't defend Geno or what happened to him. He had thought he would get him in this rehab because he knew the district attorney in Westboro. Shame on him.

Since there were no available rehabs in Massachusetts, Geno actually came up with the idea of home arrest himself. A fellow inmate had told him about it while he was in the holding area in Westboro. Geno suggested it to the lawyer.

So much for this Boston lawyer; criminals seemed a little more informed.

So, it was agreed; my son would be on home arrest with a GPS tracker for three months.

I was thrilled. I didn't think he was a kid who could stay in jail. When I had visited him prior to his sentencing, he had mentioned they were letting him vegetate in a jail cell with a child molester.

Of course, he freaked out, considering he had been molested as a child.

Maybe I was wrong, maybe we should have left him in jail, but it just didn't feel right. Staying with us on home arrest seemed the correct avenue to take.

We really didn't know, Gary and I were never involved in this world before.

But it seemed better than jail where he could be abused or become a criminal.

CHAPTER 31

HOUSE ARREST

Having Geno at home on house arrest was a big mistake.

What was explained to us was, that Geno had to stay home with a GPS 24 hours a day except when he was with the sheriff's department in Lowell where he spent from 9 to 3 every day. When he was in Lowell he attended classes on drug awareness safety, etc. He needed a ride there until he could prove he could be trusted taking a bus.

For three weeks, I drove him and picked him up. I had to make arrangements with my job, but was grateful my boss went along with it.

He seemed to be getting a lot of good information on recovery; the teachers or counselors (not sure of their title) were wonderful to him. He did the counseling part three days a week, the other two days he had to do general work, such as cleaning up trash on the side of the road, mow lawns, work in a nursing facility, as least that is what Geno told me.

When I drove him to Lowell in the morning we listened to the radio and talk shows. We frequently changed stations but we both liked hearing "Matty in the Morning" or KISS 108.

Matty and his crew had us in hysterics but in between the talk the station played lots of tunes, mostly from the present.

Geno loved the song by Lukas Graham that began, *"When I was seven years old, my mother told me..."* He would sing it over and over in a horrible voice, but by the end of six weeks I loved his voice, only because it was a happy voice.

I thought my son was getting better.

At the sheriff's office in Lowell Geno had to be drug tested daily. He always passed. But after three weeks of his being there I could tell he was high on something.

I confronted him and he denied it.

"Stop focusing on me, Mom, I am not getting high!"

But of course, he was, I knew from personal experience but I was hoping they would notice at the sheriff's office.

One day I drove him there at 9 in the morning and he was stoned on something. I watched him stagger into the office where they held classes. I said nothing as I watched his unsteady gait. One of his buddies opened the door for him, laughing. I was furious — he was taking me for a fool! I picked him up at noon, hoping they would keep him because any person in their right mind would know he was stoned.

I remembered what my sister Irene told me about the whizzinator, so I passed the information on to the sheriff's office. It was old news there. Massachusetts was evidently a bit ahead of the west coast in that respect.

He walked out of the building as if nothing was wrong.

Geno kept badgering me, trying to make me look like I was the one at fault and that there were no drugs in his system.

Time passed; I decided to just shut my mouth and see what would happen with Geno through the court system.

He had gotten permission to take public transportation to Lowell. I would drop him off at the bus stop in Billerica or the bus stop at Lahey Clinic that went to Lowell.

Geno was up and down, very straight or very high. He was manipulating the counselors. He got away with it, maybe because he was a lovable kid with a bachelor's degree from a reputable college and had been a hockey champ at one point in his life.

But he fooled them; one of the counselors told him he should be doing his job.

It was the end of April 2016. He now had permission to work, which he did. He was never lazy and wanted to get back to the Geno he was at 25, or so he told me.

"I'll never get Heather back, she's such a good woman, Mom, and she'd be afraid I'd use drugs again.

I had nothing to say; I would have done anything humanly possible to make my son stop using; but I knew that wouldn't work and wasn't the answer.

I was frightened for his life every time he left my sight. Some days he was the kid we brought up and others he was a classic addict — not happy, seeking any kind of drug he could get his hands on.

On Tuesdays' he worked on the side of a road picking up trash. If that isn't humbling I don't know what is.

I took the opportunity to call the sheriff's office and try to find out what drugs they were testing for.

"Oh, Mrs. Genovese, we check for a quantity of drugs. He named everything in the world but fentanyl. Oh, and methadone — but you can't get high on methadone."

"Really?" I said. "Are you kidding me? Methadone, you can get high on, believe me, from past experience it's a drug that can mess you up."

"But…but," the counselor was trying to get a word in to defend the state of Massachusetts, but I had the louder voice and I was going to use it!

"Kids are dying from fentanyl overdoses daily, and your department is not testing for that?"

"They are expensive drugs to test, Mrs. Genovese."

"So, money is more than a kid's life?" Shame on you and the sheriff, and all the politicians that decided on this rule. I want a call back from the sheriff!"

My heart ached but I was furious; I needed to talk to someone high in command. Who could I call that would listen and care. I figured the sheriff would not return a crazy mother's call.

Two men, both addicted to opioids in the sheriff's program, used intravenous fentanyl and had died a few days before. Geno knew them and went to their wake.

My son had no intentions of dying; he wanted to get well. He cried when those buddies of his died. I had to do something. Even if it amounted to nothing, I would get this off my chest, so once again I spoke to the secretary at Lowell, who told me Middlesex County Sheriff Peter Koutoujian was not available. I gave her my information and told her my concerns. She said he would definitely call me back. I prayed, I hoped he would and he didn't. My son was just another statistic with a crazy mother.

Maybe he was hoping I would get tired of trying to reach him, and tired I did get, but I didn't lose my will to keep my son and other addicts alive. If I could talk to the DEA (drug enforcement agency) who I called but got nowhere, anyone who would listen to get drug testing for fentanyl and methadone as part of their screening, maybe lives could be saved.

I thought of a state senator from Watertown where I grew up. He was involved in committees for addiction recovery. I gave him a call. He had just resigned from being on the drug enforcement committee as a state senator, he took a job as a union leader, but when I told him my son's story he wanted to help. He would try.

If my dad were alive, well, so many people owed him political favors that Geno would probably have gotten to that rehab in Florida where we wanted him to go.

CHAPTER 32

NO RESPONSE

Sheriff Peter Koutoujian never returned my calls, as I had mentioned. But after Geno died I received a letter of their concern, offering his condolences and asking for my input on addiction.

Thanks, but your letter came too late; my son was dead. Did you hear me??? Dead, off this earth. If the government didn't worry about money and drug testing, Geno would be alive.

Two days after Geno's death, the state of Massachusetts, passed a bill to check urine and blood samples in all drug clinics for Fentanyl which was the ingredient added to heroin.

Thanks a lot, but really, shame on all or most of the politicians that didn't care what was tested, who was tested, as long as it wasn't their own child.

Who really cares? This disease is complicated, painful and in the end, 90% of addicts die. I am not kidding; that kind of percentage should piss people off.

It does for a moment. They read the *Boston Globe* or any other major paper in the United States for a minute, and they may get mad, furious. But they look at the clock and realize they have to get to work, or get their kids to baseball practice or a hockey game and the idea of addiction ever happening to their child goes out the window.

I know because I was one of those parents. Involved in all sports with my kids.

We brought them up to be good kids, contributing members of society and hopefully they would never do drugs. I guess I was in denial, thinking if my kids were involved in activities such as sports or volunteered in their community they would be okay. For a long time, I didn't understand it was a disease that would kill, or a disease at all.

Boy, was I wrong, me and a million other parents who were too involved with trying to get their kids into good colleges, visualizing a scholarship to some Ivy League school on a sports or merit scholarship, never realizing that their child might be a future drug addict, stealing from family and friends. Incarceration wasn't in their consciousness.

Gary and I talked to our kids about drugs including alcohol and the detrimental aspects of these substances. We never expected them to be addicts, they should follow the golden rule; that was before we realized what an insidious disease addiction is, how it can easily take over your world, a world that was once beautiful and full of hope.

Looking back to the time our daughter Jessie Kate was born in 1977, then Daniel in 1979 followed by Christopher (Geno), I was so grateful for the many happy years we had. Gary and I never minded working hard, working extra shifts that would benefit our kids in athletics, academics and traveling; and I am grateful to God that he gave me three beautiful kids to add to this crazy world.

When our lives started to change in 1994 we had no idea we would have to face sexual abuse and addiction with our kids and how Gary's and my love for one another could bring us through such turmoil. When Geno entered college we thought it was over, we might get a break because God must know we were weary and getting older, and I — I won't say we, because Gary had a feeling Geno might not make it out of his addiction — that we would catch a break.

CHAPTER 33

DRIVING GENO

I finally learned to accept that this was my world with Geno when he was on house arrest. I got to know my son and he understood me as we traveled on Route 3A into Lowell every day. There was a lot of love flowing, our dog Frankie sitting in the back seat, happy to be with us and seeming to understand our conversations.

We had long talks. Geno and I had a loving connection with each other, starting at birth, continuing with Dunkin Donuts and getting to know the crew that worked there when he was 3, right through his elementary and middle school years, telling me stories I had never heard or didn't remember. We had fun as mother and son, though making the decision to let him go to a private school, a boarding school, always bothered me.

"Oh, Mom no! I loved Governor Dummer and the friends I met there."

"Imagine me not having Brian Gallagher in my life or Jen and George?"

I thought of Jen, she could really keep him on track, not to mention his coaches in hockey and football.

I cried as I was dropping him off in front of the sheriff's department.

"Don't cry, Mom, I hate when you cry."

"Well I was thinking of your high school years and how much I loved your games of my meeting Sara Morrissey. We have become such good friends."

Geno laughed. "At the hockey games, both of you had to stand right next to each other in the rink; if either of you moved it was bad luck."

I pictured Sara and me freezing in that rink, wanting to go into the ladies room because it was the only warm place.

"Mom, all those surgeries would have killed my spirit, the only reason I didn't give up was because of all the encouragement I received from my teammates, their Moms and Dads, and of course the coaches; they kept me on track and from giving up."

But really? Who can keep a person with a drug addiction on track except that person themselves.

Frankie jumped out of the car and wanted to go in the building with him. Geno was such a gentle soul; he loved that dog more then he loved himself.

Frankie licked him goodbye and I watched him look at Geno as he waved goodbye to him.

On the way back to Woburn I thought of his college years.

And there was his girlfriend Heather at Assumption College. I thought they would marry someday, especially after so many years together. But once again the devil took hold of my son. I believe all opioids are related to the devil, no one could stand seeing him fade as a proud athlete and loving friend, son, brother and nephew, especially Heather. It just broke her heart.

The ones that stayed by him were the true blues, as I called them before. They loved him no matter what and stood by him. Timmy Clark the most of anyone. He never gave up hope, nor his parents Diane and Dan in the last few months of his life. Heather and Brian Gallagher as well as Jen reached out to him frequently and I was one of those true blues but I did more damage than good by enabling him at times— Gary and Jessie tried to make him better but it just didn't work. And of course his loving aunts, my sisters Kerry, Irene, Denise and Janet and my brother John and his wife Carol, but ultimately it was Geno that had to make Geno better.

John came over one day when Geno was on house arrest. He brought some sandwiches and tried to support him in a tough way. They couldn't sit in the backyard because the GPS would go off and the police would come, so they sat in the front lawn, as it was a beautiful day. If you drive by our house you will see his chair still remaining there; it was his favorite spot when he was on house arrest. I think we will leave it there in memory of my son.

Even though Geno couldn't help himself he helped so many others. That was his way, he listened to his friends, tried to fix their problems and forgot about his own needs in the long run.

Often times I would hear him on the phone, giving advise to another addict that seemed sensible and realistic; if only he could have applied it to himself.

CHAPTER 34

TRYING TO WORK, APRIL 2016

Geno tried to get his job back selling life insurance but he needed a car once again and of course he would need to be home before 10 at night. That position was out of the question, so he was out of a job. He would have to find something else, something that would let him leave the work place when he was called for a urine screen. He would be gone for an hour or two, depending on where the job was located.

He had high hopes. He would be off house arrest in early May, then he could find a job that was a little more liberal; a job that may give him a little leeway for drug tests every day and curfews.

Geno did some research from his old days at Molding and Millwork; there was a lumber company in Woburn that bought products from them and he was friendly with the owner and had a lot of respect for him.

The next day Geno called the owner and set up a time to meet with him.

We awoke to a beautiful spring morning. Geno was singing while he made scrambled eggs; for once, in a very long time he seemed happy.

Geno took the train to Lowell to see his counselor, from there he was headed to the lumber company for his interview.

I prayed all day he would get the job. I told Geno to be as honest as he could about his past and to ask them to please give him a chance.

He asked me to pick him up at their meeting place at a restaurant in North Woburn.

I said the rosary (boy, am I Catholic at times!) that he would get the job.

Geno came out all smiles!

"I got the job mom, with the stipulation I am off home arrest by May 16, my discharge date."

Things were looking up. We had friends over and a cookout that night. I drove my son to work every morning and he was able to take the train to Lowell for his drug test during his lunch break.

The bad thing was, he never knew when he had to be tested for drugs. It could be any day of the week before 2 p.m. or not at all.

The company put up with him having to leave for a couple of hours and then he tried to work late to make up the time.

His court date was set for May 14, 2016. Freedom! He would be off house arrest. They even gave him his paperwork.

But two days later there was a glitch. Sandra McNabb, his probation officer in Westboro checked one of his past urine tests and there was a question of drugs. Between Sandra, the judge and Geno's public defender, they thought it was best for him to stay on house arrest.

We were devastated. God, could you not give the Genovese family a break?

The next morning Geno went into work and for two days, he wasn't checked for drugs, but that didn't last long. The following week he had to go to Lowell, still with his GPS on and be tested for yet another three months.

Yes, another 90 days of the same old shit; Geno was still in the system.

Although Geno was a hard worker he had to keep leaving during the day. His boss called him into the office, told him how much he cared about him, but he had to temporarily let him go. He needed someone from 7 a.m. to 6 p.m. with no interruptions. His manager told him to touch base with him in three months after his next court appearance.

Geno tried to hold it together, truly he did but I saw the tears when I picked him up in north Woburn. He was silent most of the way home until we reached the traffic on Cambridge Street in Burlington.

He reached in his pocket and pulled out a five- dollar bill. He wrote something on it and when we passed the homeless person begging for money, Geno tossed him the bill.

The red light let up and Geno leaned out the window screaming "don't do drugs." They both gave each other the thumbs up.

"Generous of you, Geno."

"Pay it forward, Mom."

Really, I said to myself. I thought pay- it forward was when something good happened to you and you paid it forward- did my son really believe this was a good outcome?

CHAPTER 35

MEMORIAL WEEKEND

It was heading toward Memorial Day. I really needed something to do for the weekend, get out of dodge. My brother asked my sister Kerry and me to go up to his house in Eastman, New Hampshire; swim in the lake, shoot some pool, watch the Red Sox. I wanted to go badly but was afraid Geno might have a horrible relapse and not make it through.

I had to think about it. When I got home Wednesday night, Geno greeted me with a big smile.

"I got a job at the replacement window place in Woburn, just answering phones from 2 in the afternoon till 10 at night."

I didn't want to disappoint him, destroy his happiness, and when I heard him talk to some of his friends I did feel relieved.

"How will you get there when I'm not around to drive you?"

"I just bought rollerblades online — they will be here tomorrow."

I was a bit skeptical but I wanted to believe the best was yet to come.

"Wow — fulltime, 2 to 10?"

He nodded with such enthusiasm, there was no way I was going to let that kid down.

But he could tell, Geno knew me and my feelings.

"Don't worry Katie, this is temporary. I'll be back in the game of triple figures before you know it!"

I could have cared less about that; I wanted him to work on his sobriety.

His size 11 roller blades arrived via Amazon Thursday night, May 27.

Timmy Clark came by; looking in Tim's eyes I could tell how happy he was for his best buddy.

And Emma! Tim's daughter, started jumping up and down as she watched Geno put on his skates and head down our street, showing off a bit to the younger kids.

***

Ironically enough, after Geno died one of the neighborhood boys who was about 18 told me how much they all loved Geno and how he made the teenagers make a promise not to mess up their lives with dope.

Amazing that he could get to these kids but not to himself — what a powerful illness.

***

Geno looked sad when we went shopping for work clothes the next day. He found a few pairs of shorts, socks and shirts. He looked sad again.

"I have taken a nosedive in all the worlds I lived in."

We were in Old Navy, sorting through clothes. He shook his head; I am a total mess-up, Mom."

Tears came to his eyes. "I have gotten fired from Molding and Millwork, the best and happiest job I had, because of drugs. I lost Heather, the light of my life, Heather and her family loved me so much mom, imagine what they think of me now, and stealing money from my own brother who will never talk to me again."

There was silence.

"Slowly pay him back Geno, you'll get it paid off."

He laughed.

"In 50 years, unless I become a millionaire."

'Talk to Dan, work out a payment agreement."

"He won't go for it, he hates me and no one could blame him."

"We're family, he will understand eventually."

"Doubt it, but okay, Mom."

"And as for Heather; she adored you and she will always be there for you in a different way, in time, that pain will pass. God knows I went through many love losses so I know what I am talking about."

"Who broke your heart Mom? For some reason, I thought you only had dad in your life and the boyfriend from high school who went to Vietnam."

I laughed, counting in my head all the boys that broke my heart and soul, everyone except my wonderful husband — God was good, tossing the others out of my life so I would end up with Gary!

Later that night Geno talked to Timmy. He was upbeat and Geno always gave him advice about his marriage. His daughter Emma loved Geno. He thought of having his own Emma someday when he could get himself together and find a girl who would love him with all his flaws and family problems.

I started off to go food shopping a few hours later. I actually wanted to be on my own but Geno and doggie Frank hopped in the car.

"Hey, can we go for a ride, Mom?"

"Of course, kiddo, where to?"

Governor Dummer; I'd like to walk around the campus."

"You want your high school memories back?"

We started at the administration building and worked our way to his first dorm, then his second. But he really wanted to go back to the rink. It was closed. But we both got out of the car and just looked at the outside. It was a worn and shattered old building from the 1800's. How they had maintained it as a hockey rink I'll never know.

Memories came flooding back. The first night dropping him off at his dorm in the ninth grade — I was so homesick for him!

Frankie beside us, was looking for good grass to relieve himself.

We laughed.

"Any regrets?"

"No, I loved this place."

We meandered along the rest of the walkways and campuses to where he took classes.

"I kissed Jen for the first time in front of the library."

"She was a sweetheart of a kid, Geno. Puppy love, your first love."

"Jen was a hoot; we all had such good years here, Mom!"

"Tell me more."

He looked at the parking lot; "my first accident — I hit the math teacher's car."

"I don't remember that."

"Dad didn't want you to know."

I kicked my feet along the walkway to the football field thinking of my own good times from a parent's perspective.

We looked at his junior year dorm.

"Boy do I miss, JR."

"How did Brian get that name?"

Geno laughed; "Mom, I told you, JR is a nickname from the show "Dallas"—the main character was JR and always wore a Texas hat just like Brian. Brian looks like a big Texan!"

"He is like a brother to you, don't you think?"

"Always and forever; along with Surette, Quigley, Charlton and so many more.

I looked at him, missed my step and tumbled a bit down the hill towards the 50-yard line.

We both laughed uncontrollably!

I cleaned the branches and leaves out of my hair.

"What I was going to say is how men always call each other by their last names or nicknames."

"Chicks don't do that, right, Mom."

I smiled thinking of high school and how my girlfriend Nancy and we called each other Batman and Robin. Then, much later, my friend Judy and I referred to each other as Thelma and Louise; briefly thinking of taking off on our husbands when we were in our thirties. Then I thought of my son Dan.

"Can you make amends? To your brother, is it in your heart?"

"Mom, I would do anything to get Danny back Even though he pestered me as a kid he also taught me a lot. He loved to read. My friends would call him "Dictionary Dan.""

"I remember that! Between periods in hockey he would look up words in the dictionary and not pay attention to the coach; that pissed Marty Pierce off! Good old Marty, coach of Matignon High school for 30 years!"

I looked at my watch; traffic would be starting.

"We should head home, Geno, traffic will be brutal if we wait." When we hopped in the car, my son asked if we could drive through Newburyport where his friend Garrett lived; they were in the same year together. Jen, Garrett and Geno were the three musketeers during the Governor days.

The house was set back, huge, at least 20 rooms and very stately.

"Quite a pad; what do they do for a living?"

"I never asked" said Geno, "None of us cared about stuff like that when we were teenagers."

"So, you don't think they were impressed that your grandfather went to Harvard?"

"They did not believe he went there. Well, maybe Jen believed me but not sure her parents did. But they were good to me, too good. Boy, did my golf game improve while I was in high school!

It started to rain as we headed home. Near the Burlington Mall, there was yet another homeless guy holding up a sign: "Homeless vet in need of sustenance."

"No!" we both said at the same time and laughed.

***

When we got home, Geno was anxiously waiting to put on his rollerblades again. I watched as he hemmed and hawed, stuffing his big foot in the 'blade.

He got to the end of the street where a lot of the younger boys hung around, they cheered as he did some swirls to show off.

I so missed my kid's childhood days but it was time to move on and recreate my own life- I was important which was always mentioned in Alanon.

Geno came back a little lighter, a bit happier. I decided since it was Memorial Day weekend I would go up to my brother John's house in Eastman, N.H. I had to stop worrying about Geno.

"I am going to get myself together, Mom, I promise. No more drugs."

Geno was 30 going on 15, brilliant on one hand, yet how stupid could he be? Many times, I wanted to scream at him out of sheer frustration, and sometimes I did. As much as I told myself it was a disease, I wondered why he couldn't take the medicine, suboxone which didn't get you high but kept the opioid craving away.

His cell phone rang and off he went into the other room. Gary looked at me as if he should ask who it was.

I mouthed, "Leave it alone."

The next day Geno said he was going bowling at the new lanes in Burlington. He had a date and we had his money. He asked for some.

"Not sure honey, we worry."

"You need to trust me, Mom, I'll be okay — new job and all."

"Like that really means something Geno? A nice last high before you start another job."

I could tell he wanted to scream at me; his face turned red and he pushed the front door open angrily.

I looked outside and he was sitting on the lawn smoking a cigarette. I joined him and lit one up myself. Occasionally we'd have a butt together but I was definitely over smoking cigarettes. I pretended to inhale but never did. Four months before I had taken a cigarette from one of my friends at a party. I became nauseous and dizzy. That part of my life was over, so I fake-smoked with my son. Maybe he could relate more to me? Doubtful.

But we sat and talked. Gary said he would give him $40 and I handed him a pack of Marlboros, forgetting he could sell them for some kind of drug.

I remember my mother, who was not a smoker when I was little, suddenly starting to smoke a cigarette at the kitchen table after dinner or functions she went to. My mom apparently felt like she was in the "in crowd," in those days, puffing away and not inhaling.

I did it that night on the front lawn because it was a 10-minute time window with Geno. What I wanted was to have time with my son, a conversation at any expense.

I remembered my mother's response as she watched our reaction to her cigarette smoking, "Don't worry, girls, it's fashionable, but I never inhale."

I started laughing to myself at the vision.

"What's so funny?" Geno wanted to know.

"Memories of your grandmother smoking, trying to act cool."

Geno looked at me, being his very intuitive self.

"You're smoking butts for me, it's our chance to talk."

Fair enough.

"So who is this girl you are going out with?"

"I told you, a local." I had to let it go there.

I stood up, brushing off the cigarette ashes.

"I am going to John and Carol's for the weekend with Auntie Kerry. Dad's staying home."

"Why, to monitor me?"

"No, he is going to plant the flowers he bought."

"We laughed, remembering the time he came home, his truck full of plants from the Lexington cemetery, plants left past the date allowed after memorial day. My husband is a great gardener, beautifying our front and back yard every spring. He received so many compliments from friends and neighbors- did he pick the wrong profession?

"No Kate, it helps me relax" and we could tell it did as me and the kids would watch him digging at the earth, placing the flowers and plants perfectly in place, the correct colors all in order.

CHAPTER 36

HEADING NORTH, FRIDAY AFTERNOON

I ended up going to Eastman the following afternoon.

My brother-in-law Kenny dropped Kerry off at my house. The plan was that I would drive her car because of her neck surgery. We were both looking forward to heading to New Hampshire.

Geno came outside and kissed Kerry and me goodbye; he looked at his dad as Gary started to give him a hug.

"Hey Dad, you'll be with me all weekend — we can hug later."

We all laughed.

Geno sat on the front lawn with Frankie, holding up the retriever's paw and waving to us as we were backing out of the driveway.

I thought of stopping and taking a picture of Geno and Frankie as my son held his paw up, waving goodbye. But for some reason I didn't but wish I had, for it would be the last time I saw Geno alive.

As peaceful as it was driving up there, having a wonderful conversation with my sister, the traffic started to pick up and we almost got killed by some guy in his Beamer, switching lanes much too quickly I had an uneasy feeling.

The guy had come within two inches of smashing Kerry's car. I got the license plate number and we called the police. We will never know what happened, but I felt like a responsible citizen.

We continued to chat about our lives growing up and basically happy childhoods. We were happy to pull into my brother's driveway in New Hampshire- John greeted us with hugs and telling us what a great meal he had prepared for dinner.

CHAPTER 37

SUNDOWN AT THE LAKE, FRIDAY EVENING

In Eastman, I threw the towel down on the sand and visualized as the kids jumped off the raft and were joking around in the water.

I looked at the swing sets, picturing Geno and his cousins pushing each other, the metal chains clanking, the kids asking us for money to buy ice cream.

Those days were beautiful. Geno at 10 was amazing. He was happy and joyful and loved my brother's house at Eastman, always asking to go and play golf or beat us in a Scrabble game.

There were beautiful memories from season to season at Eastman — hiking in the woods, road races and swimming for miles. It was our home away from home.

My son Dan ran several road races at Eastman and came in first in a couple of them.

He found a girlfriend that summer and they would go to Eastman Lake and kiss on the boat while his cousin Andrew talked to some of the other girls that were hanging around the bonfire.

The memories of Eastman were wonderful and there hasn't been a season spent there that I haven't appreciated my brother John and Carol's generosity.

As the years went by and the awareness of my brother Barry's sickness came forth, it took its toll on our family and we were together less and less.

My daughter pressed charges against Barry, and it was as if she was pressing charges against my mom as well.

Sides were taken and I didn't talk to my mom for a year; she was so upset. I think she wanted us to do what Whitey Bulger's family did, pretend it didn't happen. To her, our family was as thick as blood.

My own family with Gary was solid, but my family of origin was divided. Barry was sick and needed hospitalization or jail. We all instinctively knew what was right, as damaging as it had been.

My parents have both passed away, and Barry is hospitalized.

I sat there reflecting for two hours, I realized as I glanced at my watch. The sun was low in the sky. Dinner would soon be ready.

When I arrived back at the house, my brother had delicious appetizers and a glass of Chardonnay as we waited for dinner.

"Do you think Geno will stay at this job, Kate?" my brother John asked me.

"It's a stepping stone Johnnie, I really want Geno to get help for his addiction, but he thinks work will be his rehab. He thinks if he can keep busy, be with normal kids, he'll be fine. I'm worried Johnnie, but he's 30. I can't hover, he needs to grow up and grow out of the drugs he's using."

"I'll have him talk to my friend Mike; he might be able to help him find a job more in his field."

"He has a disease Johnnie, the disease most of our relatives have. He has to dig deep into his feelings, get to the root of his problem, which I believe is his use of drugs. He is escaping from reality because of the sexual abuse not only to him but also seeing what happened to Jess and Dan. He grew up a lot in those years."

I brought up my nephew Casey, who had died of an overdose eight years before. John had tears in his eyes as I mentioned Casey. We all loved Casey so much, and the thought of losing another kid in the family from drugs was abhorrent. I prayed that the God I believed in wouldn't do that to our family, another child dead from this horrible disease. Casey and

Geno were such good buddies. We all took Casey's death hard and then, three weeks later my nephew Paul died of heart disease, but it was also a result of his addiction.

If God did this to me again, would I ever forgive him? My anger was intense.

I had grown closer to God and he had been my focus for the last 20 years. Not that I went to any particular church, but at that point I decided it was time to develop my spiritual connection and follow the path of having a higher power. That was the way I brought my kids up. It was important to me that my children had some kind of faith and that none of us are in charge, only God is.

Of course, it didn't particularly work out quite that way, but I did what I could while they were children and then adolescents. I knew it was important, but I let it go when they made their confirmation in the Catholic Church. I knew it was the right thing for them—and for me—they were adults and had to find their own spiritual way in this world.

My sister-in-law Carol, who is so close to me that I think of her as my sister, knew I was feeling sad. She could pick up on my vibes that afternoon.

She was trying to cheer me up. "Scrabble game, anyone?"

We all laughed. That's what Geno had said since the age of 7. He loved to play and was extremely competitive.

We all laughed and pulled out the Scrabble board.

Carol won, which clearly made her happy. She was competitive herself, though purposely let the kids win when they were little.

"I'm going to call Gary, then I'm going to bed."

It was early, but my body felt old and my mind needed a rest from worrying.

Gary answered and I could pick up something was off, even though he told me all was well.

He'd picked Geno up at the bottom of the hill around 9:45 p.m. His curfew was 10 since he had the GPS on — they had changed it the week before and he no longer was restricted to being home at 6. In hindsight, would it have made a difference?

He hated that police monitor ankle bracelet he was required to wear. It drove him crazy mentally and plus it gave him a rash. Geno was so disturbed they increased his house arrest for another three months when he felt they were wrong in doing so.

Gary told me he and Geno talked for a while when they got home.

"He said he had gone bowling and seemed happy, Kate."

I pictured him walking up Revere Road with his ankle bracelet rubbing at his skin, discouraged, wondering where his life was headed.

But that was my imagination. I hoped Gary was right and I needed to let Geno's problems be Geno's problems.

"Should I call him, Gary?"

"He seems good, Kate, He's with Frankie in the den watching a movie."

We ended our conversation.

I got under the covers and turned the light on, trying to ignore the urge to call Geno.

Gary said he was fine, I realized I had to stop smothering my son with calls.

I knew I was the sick one, at times sicker than Geno. As much as I knew it was important to his development as an adult and his recovery from the addiction to detach, I had so much trouble doing it. Thank God for Al-Anon for teaching me that lesson. I knew I needed more meetings.

I decided to go to sleep. I closed my book and shut out the light. I felt I had done the right thing this time for not interfering with my son's life.

CHAPTER 38

TRYING TO SLEEP, FRIDAY NIGHT

I kept falling in and out of La-La Land. Usually in New Hampshire I would collapse into bed at night, read a little and soon my eyes would start to close — before I knew it I would hear the birds singing and the morning light shining through the upstairs window.

I turned the light on and off, reading a little here and there. The book in my hand was one of the spiritual books I throw into my bag when I go away one I read when I can't sleep.

My mother was big on telling us stories of the saints when we were little.

I loved hearing about St. Teresa, the Archangels and all the angels that guarded the entrance to heaven, wearing their magnificent sparkling clothes that glittered in the night.

My mind went to all the years we had come here to John and Carol's house. There was Mr. Twister, the enormous tree that looked like the tree in the Rapunzel story. We would make sure we got a picture of every kid sitting on Mr. Twister, it had a different meaning for each one of them.

I still couldn't fall asleep; neither could my brother John. I heard him clear his throat and turn the TV on late into the night.

CHAPTER 39

MY WORLD ENDS, VERY EARLY SATURDAY

I was FINALLY drifting off, feeling that wonderful fogginess of sleep coming on.

I don't know how long I was asleep when I heard my cell phone ring.

There was no doubt it was bad, bad news, a call in the middle of the night.

Please, God, no—not one of my kids or Gary.

I soon answered it. I could tell by the breathing it was my daughter.

"Jess?"

"Geno is dead, Mom."

I looked at the time: 2:21. "Are you sure, honey?"

She cried out, "Of course I am sure!"

"Of course you are, honey, please put Daddy on the line. Jess, I love you."

I could still hear her sobbing, and Frankie barking in the background.

I heard other voices, it was probably the police.

I could tell Gary was crying.

"What happened, hon?"

He was gulping with sobs; his heart was breaking. "We were talking for an hour when he got home, he wasn't high, seemed OK."

"Just tell me please, Gary; how did he die?"

"I am so tired, Kate. Can we talk in the morning? He overdosed. What more is there to say?"

"I'm coming home now! I can't stay here alone without you!"

It hit me. Geno was in his heavenly realm.

My brother John took the phone from me. I heard parts of their conversation. My brother had tears in his eyes as he hung up.

"None of us can drive tonight, Kate. We'll leave in the morning."

Someone else made the decision for me.

Kerry had a Valium and gave me one. We lay on the bed together and said the rosary. We even got in all mysteries before dawn.

CHAPTER 40

THE MORNING AFTER, SATURDAY

I cannot explain how my heart felt. I wanted to die right along with my son. He was my youngest and it was too unfair to die at the age of 30, of an unintended overdose.

He was doing so well! Improving daily. I do not know what made him go out and get drugs that night — the evilness of fentanyl and heroin. The demons who sold the drugs. The person who sells these drugs should be shot, condemned to hell — they didn't care, they were killing people every day.

They were mostly men, it seemed. Maybe they were fathers with addiction problems, or husbands who were trying to stop their useless drug participation as it was slowly killing them and their families emotionally.

Eventually 5:30 arrived. Carol put on a pot of coffee as we all started to pack our clothes.

John's golf game would be canceled. Our shopping in northern New Hampshire wouldn't happen.

I waved goodbye to Mr. Twister and sobbed.

Carol drove my car home. No one would let me drive, although I believed at the time I could have. I started making phone calls to all of my friends at 7 a.m.. Carol thought I should wait, but why? They have been my eternal friends and I needed help when I got home.

Gary hugged me hard when we pulled into the driveway, his tears flowing down my neck because he couldn't stop crying. What father who loved his son could?

Friends arrived at 7:30 am with food and coffee. I felt comforted by all of the people that stopped by.

Neighbors were shocked and the kids were crying. Geno was the love of the neighborhood, he cared about everyone.

Of course, I remained in a daze. My doctor prescribed Ativan to help me relax and I was careful not to take too many.

I kept an eye on Jessie, she loved her brother so much.

We couldn't make contact with our son Dan. He lived in Moscow and the number and address we had for him was not the current one.

Flowers were ordered and we decided on a Christian burial but to be cremated.

The blessed people at the Lynch-Cantillon funeral home in Woburn were wonderful. They seemed genuinely overcome with sadness for us.

My sister Irene was called; she was supposed to come to Boston in two weeks for my brother John's 75th birthday party, but came earlier for her 30-year-old nephew's wake and burial.

Janet as well, my oldest sibling, would be coming the day of the wake.

When Irene arrived, she stayed with me. Pictures of Geno's life was being put together as well as a slideshow.

I don't know how I emotionally handled all of this but I did. It was through the grace of God and the Holy Spirit, my mother would have said.

Friends from Woburn, his Governor Dummer friends and his Assumption College buddies; not to mention all of the hundreds of people he met along the way in his short but distinguished life, all came or called to help us through.

So many of us laughed, cried, danced, telling Geno stories from the last 30 years.

I felt grateful that Gary and I were blessed with so many friends who came to our rescue.

The wake was a long six days away. It was Memorial weekend and nothing could happen until after Monday.

Geno's body was taken into Boston somewhere and I couldn't see him until he was at the funeral home.

Gary and Jess identified him at Lahey clinic in nearby Burlington at 1:10 am on Saturday, May 28, and had called me an hour later.

Food came until our refrigerator was overflowing. It was a constant stream of friends into the house that week before the wake and burial on Thursday and Friday.

Everyone was so heartbroken.

I looked at the rollerblades he'd bought two days before to get him to work at his newest job.

Was he dead or was this a dream? The end of Christopher John Genovese's life would begin a new chapter.

***

The day before Geno died he had interviewed in Cummings Park for the job at a replacement window company. He had to go to Lowell on the train, and I waved goodbye, feeling hopeful.

His friend Timmy saw Geno walking forward to the train station; he almost stopped to ask him to go to his college reunion that weekend.

Tim said he considered asking Geno if he would like to go to Martha's Vineyard with him and his college buddies. These were people Geno already knew, but Tim said his own schedule was tight.

When Tim heard what happened to Geno he was guilt-ridden. "Why didn't I stop the car and take him with me?"

I had to tell Timmy time and again it wasn't his fault.

"He wouldn't have gone anyway, Tim. He already had a plan in his head and it involved getting high."

"But maybe I could have talked him out of it."

"That still wouldn't have worked, he had to go to see his counselor in Lowell. You would have missed the ferry."

But that same day Timmy told me a story that I hadn't heard. He had been with Geno just a few days before that, when Geno had called to ask him for a ride home from Burger King. When Timmy arrived, he said Geno was in fine form, singing the Righteous Brothers, "You've Lost That Lovin' Feeling," much to the entertainment of everyone in the place.

"Everybody loved Geno, he had such great energy, he cared about so many people and made them happy," Tim said.

But I knew how Tim felt as I had almost canceled my plans to go to my brother's house in New Hampshire , thinking Geno needed me at home. I still wanted to be that helicopter mom, but it was different, I was afraid for his life. Helicopter moms generally are watching over their 10-year-olds too intensely, making sure they were not lying. I guess they come in all ages, the mothers and the sons.

Gary said, "if you had not gone to New Hampshire you would have done the same thing I did; you would have talked to him for a while and he wanted me or you or anyone else with him to go to bed so he could get high; it wasn't your fault Kate, my fault or Timmy's either; it was God's plan."

Gary and I didn't fail as parents and Timmy didn't fail as a friend. He was going to overdose and die sooner or later if he didn't get help.

***

The system failed Geno. The court system didn't care about my son, it cared about his violating probation and fining him $300 multiple times.

No one listened to my cry for help for Geno.

"Please, he needs a rehab, not jail or a continuation of paying fines for violating probation," I would say time and time again.

I begged the judge in the Westborough court: "Please allow him to go to Florida to a rehab we found; Massachusetts has nothing available."

Geno had a list of rehabs and he called every day when he was on house arrest. It is a shame that a political state like Massachusetts had so few public health beds available for people with substance abuse disorders.

***

I finally got to see my son's dead body an hour before people arrived at the funeral home on Thursday afternoon. That morning, Gary and I had gone to Kohl's department store, searching for clothes adequate for a wake and funeral for our son. Gary searched for a shirt and tie for him.

We prayed we would hear from our son Danny in Moscow; I had this tragic feeling he didn't know his brother was dead. We had no idea Danny's size clothes but Gary took a guess at it and picked out something appropriate just in case he made it home.

I wore black and white and some silver earrings. My hairdresser gifted me with a nice hairdo.

Everything was organized. Pictures, a movie of him from birth to the end,

It was beautiful.

I saw Geno's corpse first, before the rest of the family.

"Katie," my sister Renie said, and walked me over to the casket.

Geno looked like he was smiling. Vestiges of freckles were on his nose and his dimples were showing slightly.

I leaned over and kissed his cold cheek.

My son, our athlete, our soldier in Christ.

I tried not to cry but I did. I sobbed hard for 10 seconds, then Karen, one of the school nurses I had worked with came and hugged me; her grandfather was being waked there as well.

"So sorry, Kate."

"Sorry to you, Karen."

"But it's different; Geno was so young."

I walked back to the casket. I wanted to jump in with him. One last hug.

I felt a hand on my back.

"Mom, people are lining up outside."

That meant *move it.*

***

I thought back to my dad's death in 1986.

My sister Irene had come in from Seattle. The two of them had had a tumultuous relationship.

My dad had been emphatic in his desire for Irene to go to Trinity College in Ireland. That plan changed when Irene's boyfriend came home from a military leave in Vietnam and she became pregnant.

I remember how sad my father was at the time. I heard him sobbing and my mother trying to console him.

There would be no Trinity College but there would be a baby, our nephew Paul Jr. with his big brown eyes and red hair. Years later, that baby of Irene's would die too young himself.

My dad never quite got over his disappointment with the turn her life had taken those many years ago.

And at Dad's death she cried her eyes out and tried to climb in the casket, a real Irish wake.

"Irene," I had yelled at her. They need to brush Dad's hair, get out of the friggin' casket."

The wake brought back thoughts of my dad, and everyone in our family who was gone as well. Jessie touched my shoulder and disappeared.

Oh my God, she is leaving; she can't take it in here because she is so upset. But, no, before I could go after her she came back with Geno's sunglasses that he always wore. She placed them on his forehead.

Tears in her eyes, Jessie said, "Now that's our Geno."

CHAPTER 41

ENDINGS
AND NEW BEGINNINGS

More than 450 people arrived at his wake. I heard wonderful stories; he was truly loved.

One of his female friends told me he saved her from being attacked on their college campus; "I think I'm alive because of Geno."

He talked the dean out of throwing a friend out of school for being drunk on Campus.

He played his heart out in hockey, even if it meant taking pain killers to get through the game.

He carried his girlfriend Heather off the soccer field when she tore her ACL.

They both got a standing ovation. I pictured Geno grinning as he walked off the field, proud that he could help.

Gary's buddies from the town of Lexington came. I don't think anyone missed. So many of Gary's friends from work told me what a hard worker he was, how funny and such a good Dad.

I don't know how I didn't break into tears every few minutes; my guardian angels were by my side.

My friends from kindergarten, high school, college, places I worked as a nurse all showed up for a final goodbye to Geno.

I think every one of my neighbors came to say their farewells; some of their stories were told as they remember him growing into a nice young man.

Someone said after the funeral mass;

"You did a good job bringing your kids up!"

I smiled. I wasn't feeling very successful at the moment.

It was hard to feel miserable when our friends and family surrounded us. I squeezed a friend of mine from high school much too hard, he knew the disease way too well, but he buried his addiction, only to live to help someone else, a day at a time.

I didn't want the night to end, picturing Geno alone in the funeral home. He wasn't alone, though; God was with him.

I loved all my Al-anon friends who showed up; I couldn't possibly mention everyone's names; but they wouldn't care and it wouldn't matter to them. I mattered, and Jessie and Gary.

Family and friends came back to the house. My friends Barbara and Carol pulled the show off with plenty of food and making sure I didn't lift a finger.

Thank God Renie arrived from Oregon several days before the wake and was staying with us; but no Danny- where was my Dan?

Friends of his from high school and University of Vermont came in remembrance.

"Where's Dan? How's Dan?"

I actually couldn't remember if we found him and he couldn't come, or he had no idea his brother had died.

The next day was going to be hard; Gary and I went to bed. Friends cleaned up

Downstairs. I woke up in the middle of the night and thought I saw Geno putting a golf ball in the living room- the vision of him smiling soothed me and helped me fall back to sleep.

***

The next day, the limo picked us up at 9. I was in the back seat looking out the window; I didn't want to cry and smudge my make-up. I laughed to myself, wishing that was my biggest problem.

I leaned my head back and suddenly saw a vision of a woman I had never seen in my life. She was older, in her seventies, looking like my stern fifth grade teacher at the Lowell school. I suddenly heard her say "Your son is going to be okay." I thought I was hallucinating or dreaming, it was very strange, who was this unknown person entering my thoughts?

"Did you hear me? We will be taking care of him." Then the vision disappeared; I probably shouldn't have taken the Ativan before we left.

In the church, I closed my eyes and leaned my head on Gary's shoulder. Suddenly I saw groups of people I never saw before in my life walking in the side door of St. Barbara's; they were all joyful and smiling, but when I opened my eyes everything was normal.

"Are you okay?" Gary asked, as he squeezed my hand.

"I hope so; I feel like I'm on an acid trip."

"You're okay, Kate. It's nerves."

I wish I could say it was a beautiful service but I only remember some of it.

I do remember receiving communion, with Timmy Clark's beautiful eulogy, my family surrounding me and then the casket going down the aisle and following it, looking at our friend Chuck Toomey and squeezing his hand. At least the people I didn't know that were in my head had left!

I was so exhausted I had to lie down after the service. When I saw Geno's body being taken away and his friends watching his corpse disappearing in the black limo, it made me so sad. It was so, sad I thought that he couldn't have gotten well and continued his life like all of his friends standing around, watching his body heading off.

Watching my daughter Jessie outside of the church broke my heart. She was in tears and holding onto my husband, as if somehow hoping her wonderful dad could perform a miracle and bring Geno back.

I fell asleep for two hours. When I woke up friends, neighbors, and family were in the backyard. I was so grateful for all of his hockey, golf and football buddies, his work friends and mine, other people he met over the years who came, and teachers from kindergarten, right through his college years who came back to our house.

***

One of Geno's friends told me he had a real presence when he walked in a room and how somehow he made everyone feel important.

We all have a purpose in this world and we are all important; the trash man who gets rid of the garbage every week to the executive who has to run a company and do it honestly.

The politician who is supposed to look after their own district and even the president of the United States; we are all accountable for one another on different levels. Basically, we need to show respect for one another.

Did my Geno ever absorb any of this? I am sure he did.

I heard him giving advice to a friend who wanted to kill himself in eighth grade because his girlfriend broke up with him, later on, calling his parent.

My son made an effort to help others, just because. It was in his blood; he had a mother who was a nurse and a father who didn't leave people deserted along the side of the road.

His father taught him to give 100 percent every time he put those skates on and hit the ice, not to show off but to represent the team.

There was so much we tried to convey to our children and as I write this I don't feel very successful; yet I did my best.

Geno didn't die because of anything I did, he had a disease he couldn't get a hold of, but of course, there were mistakes I made along the way.

And Dan, my lost soul son, we can't find you but we pray every day you will understand your purpose in this world and remember your upbringing and how much we love you.

And thank God for our wonderful Jessie, our daughter who made Gary and me want to live 38 years ago. She was precious then and is precious, successful and a kind human being to this day. Her husband Bryan is a gem; I picture him hugging Jess and me, reinforcing that all will be well. God's got your back Bryan, I just know it!

Two days after the funeral we received Geno's ashes. We weren't quite sure what to do with them, so we waited.

It was the same with his clothes. His cousins and friends have looked through items and taken some of them, l thought I saw them cry when they picked them up, holding a shirt, smelling the scent of Geno.

The kids had a baseball field in our backyard. All their friends played baseball there daily for years. The Keenes, the Clarkes, and all the others who lived on the street, as well as the times when suddenly friends from other parts of the city would show up.

Gary looked out the window one day when he was doing the dishes.

"Home plate," he said, "We'll start with his ashes under home plate when the weather improves. Tears and more tears came to me. The vision of Geno playing with the whole neighborhood; and when he was 6, walking down to the Kennedys looking for Courtney, who was six years older, to play hide-and-go-seek.

Gary pitching to them, showing them how to hold a bat correctly and everyone clapping when one of them got a hit.

Yes, home plate. That's where we will start. Eventually we will put his ashes at special places and give some away to friends in little urns.

Yet this is hard work to do, maybe even more difficult than the day he died. We have to revisit his life, his clothes, shoes, pictures, trophies. That last item, that may be the hardest. Geno used to be so proud and humble when his name was called out at a hockey banquet for the MVP award or most goals for the year.

Even golf, his trophy from being on the first place team when he worked at Molding and Millwork.

Why keep all this painful memorabilia?

Maybe I will keep one or two of each of Geno's trophies for old time's sake.

I looked in Geno's room and counted 25 of them. Maybe more than one or two.

***

A few years back, Geno and I were trying to get his trophies off the shelf in his closet. The board they were on, up above the closet was weak, suddenly they came tumbling down, along with my son Dan's books from high school. Geno tried to push me away as they fell but it was too late. A dictionary that must have weighed about 100 pounds came tumbling down and hit my leg. As the night went on, Geno looked at my leg; a huge bruise was coming alive and my foot was turning purple.

My son truly felt horrible and dragged me to the emergency room where I was treated and on bedrest for four days with my foot elevated and wrapped in an ace bandage.

I watched all the books and some of the trophies that fell get hauled out by Geno and friends. Little did I know he kept some of them. He couldn't seem to part with the MVP and golf award — he said he wanted to show his kids someday, give them the incentive to be active in sports.

Friends and neighbors asked me if we knew who sold Geno the drugs. Detective John Walsh was in charge of the case, he couldn't have been nicer. After some investigating and finding out where Geno bought the heroin, he had an idea of whom it may have been. A few weeks after my son's death Detective Walsh came to our house and told us the person or persons were in jail and there wasn't much investigating he could do until they were released. I wanted to hate this person but hate just isn't in my heart; God will punish the person in some way or another.

I thanked John and the Woburn police for doing an investigation and being so kind to me and my family during our time of mourning, and I know you will do your best to help the kids with this disease and be pro-active in putting an end to substance abuse.

***

Two weeks after Geno died I got a telephone call from an agency saying I had an appointment with them for a position as a nurse who gives injections to people who travel around the world.

I didn't remember the phone call as I was in a daze, but I asked the caller to explain the job to me. It sounded simple and I needed to get my mind off of my pain.

The offices were in Woburn and Cambridge where I would divide my time.

It was a good diversion, but every day at work, when it was lunchtime, I went in my car and cried for 45 minutes. I missed my son, why did he die?

One day on the way into Cambridge I was driving down Mass Ave. The tears wouldn't stop and I felt nauseous; I pulled into a nursery where flowers were blooming and there was a man watering the greenery.

The place wasn't open yet, so I pulled into a parking space and started vomiting on the mulch in the back of the building.

I couldn't help it. I finally stopped and leaned against the car.

The man watering the shrubbery came over to me.

"Are you okay, young lady?"

I wiped my tears.

"Not really. My son died a few weeks ago and I am brokenhearted."

He looked embarrassed, didn't know what to say.

He started biting his nails, he looked nervous. "I don't think you should drive, let me call one of your friends to drive you home."

I thought of my boss, the wicked witch from the west. I had to laugh at his idea. "No, give me a few, I need to work."

I watched him walk away, continuing his work. I threw up one more time and felt better.

He came over to me and I said, "I'm sorry I puked in your mulch, can I pay you for the damage?"

He handed me a tissue and said, "Go home, my dear, that's what I suggest — but somehow I know you will go to work."

"Thanks for understanding," I told him and drove off toward Cambridge. I was a fighter, I needed to work. That's what nurses do, take care of others.

The job turned out to be good for me. I liked the clients, but my boss — not so much. I gave up the position the end of September and took a trip to Mississippi and New Orleans with my husband. The two of us needed a getaway.

My heart ached on a daily basis but I had so many friends and family to comfort me. I stayed in touch with Geno's friends and Timmy, his Mom Diane and his daughter Emma came over frequently.

Emma, who is 4 years old, looked at Geno's picture in the den.

She looked at me and said, "Geno's dead but he is in our hearts."

I smiled, well said for a 4-year-old.

Life will never be the same without my son and his beautiful soul around.

I won't hear him coming in the back door, yelling "I'm home" or running upstairs to tell me some good news.

But there was a chance he would never have recovered from his addiction. He could have continued on as an addict for the next 10 or more years, wearing us down, breaking up my marriage and all of us going insane.

So God did what he had to do, he took him home.

Once, when Geno was 3 I heard him up in his room dreaming, laughing and talking to an invisible person.

I went upstairs.

"Who are you talking to?"

"My other mother."

I curiously said, "Who could that be?"

"We lived in Michigan, she was checking on me."

I looked at him curiously, wanting to know more.

"I was a professional hockey player, I did well for a while but my other mother said I had to move on."

"So you ended up in Boston, Massachusetts"?

"My other mother told me I might be a professional hockey player when I am 18, but there was a choice I had to make."

Hockey or death due to drugs, I thought, thinking back.

I smiled and kissed him, thinking that was one hell of a dream.

Maybe there is such a thing as reincarnation. I'm not quite sure I believe in that. But one night I had a vision/dream of Geno coming to me, months after he died. He told me he was going to do it right this time, have two kids and become a lawyer.

What a wonderful thought. But I needed to heal, move on with my wonderful husband and the rest of my family. Geno will never be forgotten.

I heard a picture of him is pasted on the athletic trainer's room at Governor Dummer for being a great athlete with the most injuries in his high school years!

CELEBRATING GENO'S 31ST BIRTHDAY

We had a plaque made for Geno for the statue at Horn Pond in Woburn. The Angel of Hope is dedicated to all the children, men or women, who died before their parents. Geno is represented there now.

Several of our friends and family joined us there, along with Geno's buddies.

There were a few people who spoke of Geno and how he would be missed. I just didn't have it in me to cry. For some reason I wanted it to be the celebration of his first birthday in heaven.

We went back to our house. Jessie had bought 31 balloons. They were blue, his favorite color. His friends wrote messages on index cards and stapled them to the strings, then most of us looked up as they drifted into the unknown, into another world, another dimension, maybe to the heavenly realm, Geno's new home.

Tears were in everyone's eyes, I turned and went into my house, a home where the memories of Geno would always stay alive.

I looked at the picture of our family 25 years ago that sits on the fireplace mantel. Geno was only 6. It was the day we had gotten married for the second time; my mother got her wish, a church wedding. Remembrances flooded in of Geno in St. Barbara's taking pictures of people who came in. I heard a sudden burst of laughter; Geno was taking pictures of the stations of the cross. How adorable was, that? A little boy snapping away, asking what each station meant.

"Please take good care of him, Jesus," I whispered to myself.

Jessie hugged me. Thank God for my daughter. I am so lucky to have this kid in my life, I thought. Jessie is a gift God gave us. We didn't know if she would have two legs when she was born at the University of Washington Hospital 40 years ago! And Jessie was perfect and healthy, and turned out to be a good sister to Geno as well, maybe too good at times.

As I mentioned, Geno had wanted to write a book, his story, something like "Basketball Diaries," a true story of a kid who got hooked on drugs but loved basketball. That guy ended up writing his story in a jail cell.

It made me wonder when he was arrested last January if we should have suggested he stay in jail, maybe he would have straightened out, written a book.

But no. As tough as Geno looked, he wouldn't have survived emotionally, his heart and feelings were too tender and more than likely the prison cell would have added its own unique kind of unbearable damage.

Some friends have asked me why I wanted to write this story and expose our family, Geno's life, to the world.

My answer was I never thought of *not* writing it. His life needed to be shared with the world. The content of this book will help someone, maybe 10 or 20 but I hope many, many more.

As I am sitting in my beautiful yard typing away, there is another family experiencing what we went through and maybe our story will help them to see they're not alone with this disease.

I do not feel ashamed any longer; addiction is a disease and should be treated like one. That is my main message.

He needed a chance at working his issues out in a drug rehab instead of jail and house arrest.

Geno needed to be around professionals who knew what addiction was all about. If that had happened maybe my son might have gotten better through their help and the help of 12 step programs.

It takes a village to raise a child, as Hillary Clinton said. It is so true.

No one can fight this disease alone; most illnesses require professional help. So why didn't the judges, district attorneys, probation officers and so many others see this?

I pictured the judge and a different scenario- looking at Geno and wanting to give him another chance at life in a recovery center. It would have been a new game plan, a good solid rehab in Florida that had a history of patients making good recoveries instead of sending Geno to jail.

Geno deserved to live. He deserved a fighting chance to be able to try, to get back on his feet and have a chance at a life that might have been wonderful.

Still, he was beautiful inside and out till the day he died.

Maybe he didn't have it in him to try and make his life whole again. I think he felt he lost too much and he'd have to do a lot of scrambling around, kicking his feet, crying, begging God to get his soul back.

I guess it just wasn't in the cards for him.

In March of 2017, my former neighbor, but a friend for twenty- five years, Kathy Moore, found a letter on her front lawn. It was in an envelope sealed and addressed to Gary and me.

The envelope was from his hockey coach at Assumption College; Lance Brady.

The letter had been sitting there for months, covered with snow, dried multiple times, probably muddy and wet, but meant to be found.

A gift from God. Lance loved my son. He praised him for being a wonderful student, athlete and captain of the college hockey team.

His beautiful words were what I needed that day. I must have read that letter five times a day for weeks. What Lance wrote was clearly the essence of the life Geno led. I felt so proud Geno had accomplished so much in his 30 years on this earth. Thank you, Lance, and all the people in Geno's world over the last 30 years who loved him, respected him and who he helped along the way.

More than a year has passed at this point since Geno's death. I wake up thinking of him and turn my beloved son over to God.

The first six months I cried quite a bit, both alone, with friends, my therapist. Sometimes it was just Gary and me hugging each other and each of us feeling the other's tears.

It is normal to cry.

"If you don't cry, your organs cry," my sister Denise, a therapist, tells me. There is no shame in tears, it is better to cry out the grief and let your organs be free of diseases such as cancer, arthritis and a multitude of others. I thought of my mother; I think I saw her cry twice in my life. Once was when my dad died and the other when my brother Barry got sentenced to Bridgewater jail.

"Irish people cry a lot, Katie. The Scottish wouldn't think of it," she told me six months after my dad's passing. "Be strong," she said, "you don't want your kids to see you 'wailing.' You have a backbone."

But I didn't pay attention to her, I missed my dad and my tears over his death helped me heal.

I think my father cried more than my mom. Every Easter, he would listen to the song "In your Easter Bonnet" it must have brought memories to him of his East Cambridge days. My dad and one of his sisters lived with their grandmother in a triple decker. The children were poor, but so loved. I thought of the people I loved that have passed to the other side and I picture a heavenly party going on, with Geno dancing and his great big smile as he is relieved to be out of the pain he was in.

Some days I don't care if I live, but I don't want to die, either.

This world is still a beautiful place and God isn't finished with me yet. There is still work to be done or wonderful events still to occur.

I think of some things I would like to happen before it is my time to leave this earth. I may become a grandmother, I would like that. I haven't traveled to every state in the USA. I am not through helping my Democratic party make this country a place everyone can visit without fear. And, of course, I plan to do what I can to stop the addiction epidemic as well as sexual abuse with children.

I have been blessed with a wonderful husband and marriage. When we met 40 something years ago I didn't realize I would appreciate Gary as much as I do. He is loving, kind and loyal, not just to me but to everyone that enters his life. I have never heard him gossip or treat anyone badly. He is a solid guy.

And I am going to put every ounce of energy into making this book successful; I know it will be God's will, not mine, but I still need to do the footwork.

The tears have died down but the wonderful memories of Geno never will.

I went to church this morning. The minister of women's studies talked about endings and new beginnings, relating the story to Moses in the bible.

She is a Southern girl who moved to Massachusetts two years ago and has been very homesick, yet knowing this is the path she needs to travel.

God had me go to church for a reason, because the message today was for me. I finally feel Geno's death was an ending for me as well, yet at the same time a new beginning for him in heaven and for me on this earth without one of my children, my Geno.

And maybe, just maybe this book will help other parents and friends of Geno's in the long run. Time will tell.

I will more than likely stay on the runway called Earth for a bit longer to share with others my experience of dealing with substance abuse. The thought of being able to help one kid stay sober and take a day at a time without chemicals in their bodies, then my life will be worth living, knowing that it isn't necessary to be high on drugs to stay happy.

Godspeed.

JANUARY 14, 2017

When my sister Irene came for Geno's services she stayed another month or so. She believed her cancer was in remission and so she made a big decision, she was moving back East to be with her brothers, sisters, nieces, nephews, and old friends she had kept in touch with for the last 40 years.

Irene had gone from Seattle to Northern California. After her divorce she moved to Ashland, Oregon. She had become a real West Coaster and every time she made a visit home she couldn't wait to head back. But this time was different.

"We've had too many deaths in the family, I feel it's right to be back, I'm beginning to feel homesick for Boston."

Her two kids live in Maui with her two grandchildren. Her oldest son Paul died eight years ago. She thought of moving to Maui, but hated the heat, so through the months of August and September she packed all her belongings, sold her house, furniture, everything. She was starting over.

She visited her kids in Maui for a week and was back in Boston before the holidays in 2016.

But when she got here she started to feel sick and had horrible pain.

We found her a wonderful doctor at Lahey Clinic; unfortunately the lung cancer was back and had spread. She got a second opinion at Dana

Faber, but both agreed, saying radiation wouldn't work, she had received the maximum amount in Oregon, and they would give her maybe six months to live with chemotherapy.

I had been selfish. I begged her to try the chemo. "I can't lose you Irene, I just lost Geno," I told her.

Renie chose not to do anything except take her vitamins, eat anti-cancer foods and use all sorts of alternative treatments.

"I'm not going to die," she told me. She was convinced her alternative treatments would work.

She made it through Christmas. He lifelong friends Donna Feeley and Joan Murphy helped her right along with the rest of the family.

She stayed with my sister Kerry and brother-in-law Kenny. Hospice was called in and she eventually got sent to a hospice house where her life would end.

The family took turns staying with her and her daughter Leah came from Maui.

She took her last breath at 5 o'clock on January 14, eight months after we lost our son.

There were four different celebrations for my sister after her death, here in Boston, and the other places she lived — Seattle, Ashland and an American Native celebration in California. She was so loved by so many people and I miss and pray, talk to her every day about the wonderful memories we shared as sisters and friends.

I had a wonderful vivid dream a month after she passed. Irene was on a rope swing ready to land in the water and Geno was on the other rope swing. They were swinging back and forth. Irene was yodeling (which she learned in Oregon). Geno was laughing and smiling with a big grin, but they just kept swinging on the ropes but never landed in the water, which was the bluest water I have ever seen. Then I woke up, boo. I didn't want the dream to end, I wanted to be part of the dream for just a bit longer.

We lived together on Thayer St in Belmont. So many memories came back and the courage she had when her husband Paul, strung out on heroin took the only transportation she had, their car, or should I say his car because the government sent him 4,00 bucks and he bought a car for his family.

But when he got addicted to heroin he went to her house, made her get the title and took off with it to the VA in Boston, where he sold it for heroin.

Irene and her son Paul were carless. I was furious! Irene wasn't.

"Something good is going to come just around the corner."

I wanted to balf! My mother's saying when something didn't go your way.

But a week later, John Capuano, my brother-in-law, dropped off a brand new bike for Irene with a babyseat. Rene thought she'd died and gone to heaven!

I looked at her as if she was insane and wanted to GET BACK at Paul. But know, Irene made the best of the bike.

She drove it to her in-law's house so they could watch her son, then she worked from 4pm till 11 pm and drove the bike home. In the morning, she picked Paul up and off they would go on the bike, stopping in Cushing Square at Ohlin's bakery for a donut.

Rene didn't have a mean bone in her body, and I was more than lucky to have her in my life.

I just know Irene is having the time of her life on the other side, but oh, how we miss her beautiful spirit!

Godspeed to you as well, my dear sister.

ABOUT THE AUTHOR

Kate Genovese was born in Watertown, Massachusetts (a suburb of Boston) and was the sixth of seven children. Her parents were big on education and reading. Her father encouraged reading at least three books a month since the age of six and Kate's love for reading started then.

Kate's passion for writing didn't start until she was well into her forties. She was going through a difficult time in her life and an event occurred with her children and family of origin that led Kate to write her first unpublished book, *A Silence So Still*.

She realized the healing aspect of writing and creating characters and went on to publish three books: *Thirty Years in September; A Nurses Memoir*, which is autobiographical, *Loving Joe Gallucci*, and *Two Weeks Since My Last Confession*, which is fictional family drama.

Loving Joe Gallucci is a true love story based on the hepatitis C virus and has been made into a movie script that is being considered by directors. Some of the proceeds go to the **Liver Foundation** from the sales of the book.

Kate has been a registered nurse for over 30 years, is involved in alternative medicine and runs her own Reiki practice.

She has been married to her husband Gary for more than 35 years. They live north of Boston with their Golden Retriever Frankie.

CPSIA information can be obtained
at www.ICGtesting.com
Printed in the USA
BVHW02s0851270218
509196BV00008B/24/P